The 5(... /

B R ... E S

INTRODUCTION

Most guides take you to the same places. This book is different. It takes you to the hidden spots in Bruges almost no one knows about. It is designed to lead you away from the crowded places, to reveal the quiet canals, forgotten churches and secret alleys. It covers 500 of the city's less known spots, including a pigeon-themed restaurant, a beautiful pharmacy and a romantic cemetery.

With this book tucked in your backpack, you can set out to find unusual concept stores, secret bars with rare beers and uncommon local delicacies. It will direct you to the best places to eat authentic Belgian chips, the benches with the best views and the most beautiful cycle routes out of town.

The book doesn't tell you everything there is to see. There are already enough guide books, websites and blogs devoted to the familiar tourist places. This book goes one step further and lists the unexpected places the author would recommend to a friend who wanted to discover authentic Bruges.

You don't have to do everything listed in the book, but you should at least drink a Brugse Zot beer in one of the 5 best bars, eat at one of the 5 most romantic restaurants, and stand on one of the 5 most romantic bridges. If you do so, you will begin to understand why people have been falling in love with this small city for more than 500 years.

HOW TO USE THIS BOOK?

This book contains 500 things you need to know about Bruges in 100 different lists. Some are places to visit that lie off the beaten track. Others are random bits of information that tell you something about the city's character. The aim is to inspire, not to cover the city from A to Z.

The places listed in the guide are given an address, a district and a number. The district and number allow you to find the locations on the maps at the front of the book. The maps are not detailed enough to navigate around the city, but you can pick up an excellent free city map at one of the information offices (at 't Zand 34 and the railway station).

It's important to bear in mind that cities change all the time. The Flemish chef who hits a high note one day may be uninspiring on the day you happen to visit. The romantic hotel recommended in this book might have gone downhill under a new manager. Or the bar we praise so highly might have closed its doors. But we republish almost every year, so the content is regularly updated to reflect important changes and new trends.

This is obviously a highly personal selection. You might not always agree with it. If you want to leave a comment, recommend a bar or reveal your own favourite secret place, you can visit the website *www.the500hiddensecrets.com* or go to *@500hiddensecrets* on Instagram. You can find further hidden secrets of Bruges revealed on the website as well as information on more than 25 other cities in the *Hidden Secrets* series.

THE AUTHOR

Derek Blyth has lived in Belgium for more than 25 years. As a journalist, he has explored almost every corner of the country. Formerly editor-in-chief of the Brussels English-language weekly *The Bulletin*, he has written for *The Guardian* and *The Financial Times* and publishes his own blog at *www.mysecretbrussels.com*. He also organises walking tours that take small groups to hidden spots in Brussels, Antwerp and Ghent.

In 2012, he published a guide to *The 500 Hidden Secrets of Brussels*. An instant bestseller, it was widely praised for showing tourists and even locals a side of the city they never knew existed. He went on to publish guides to *The 500 Hidden Secrets of Antwerp*, followed by *The 500 Hidden Secrets of Ghent* and most recently *Hidden Belgium*.

The author has spent many years exploring Bruges. But he has not discovered everything on his own. He is grateful to friends, locals and random strangers who have generously shared their secrets over many years. He also owes a huge debt to his publisher Marc Verhagen and the team at Luster for putting so much effort into these guides. Thanks to their dedication, this guidebook offers a different way to discover one of Europe's most beautiful destinations.

BRUGES

overview

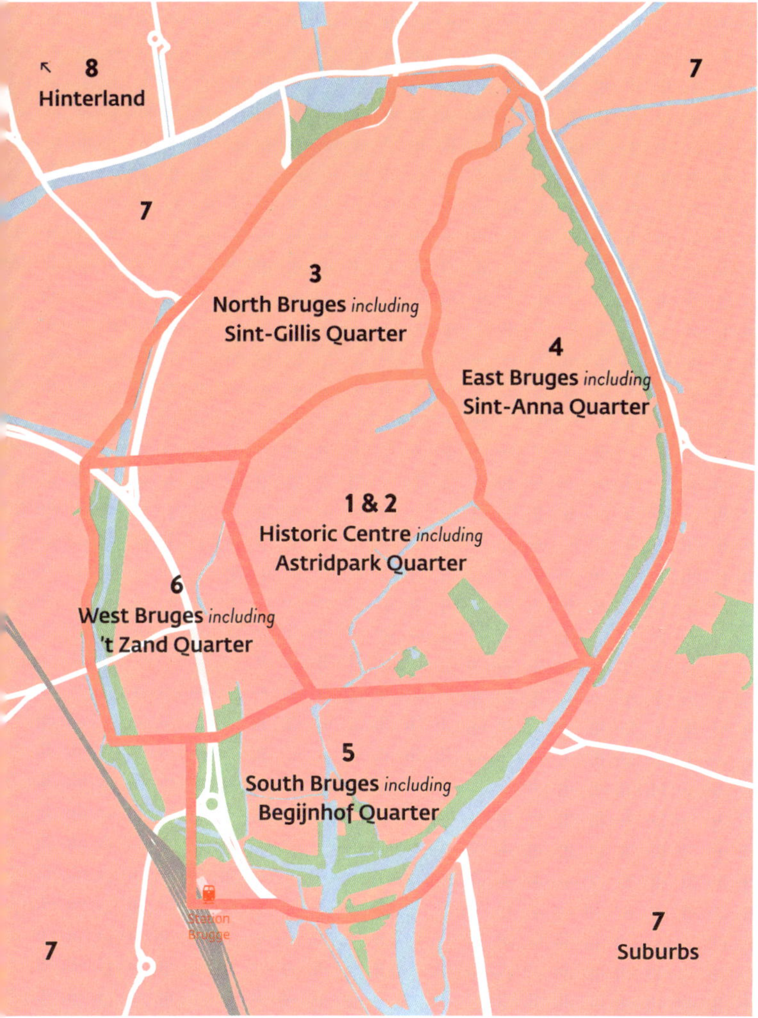

Map 1

HISTORIC CENTRE (NORTH)

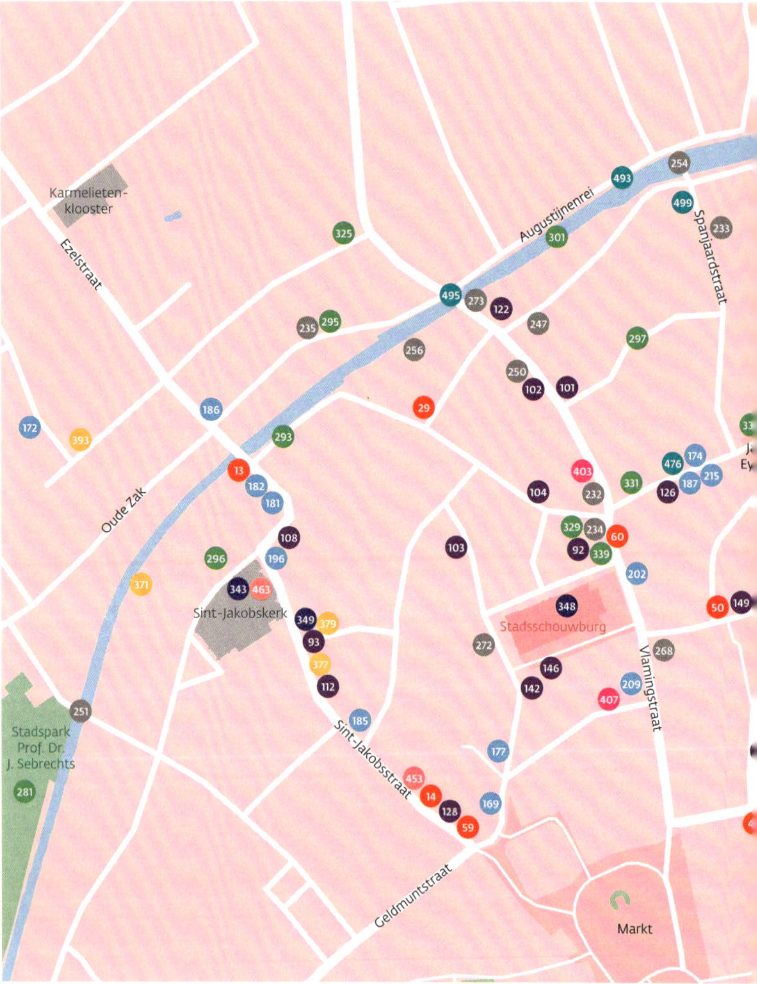

EAT – DRINK – SHOP – BUILDINGS – DISCOVER – CULTURE – SLEEP – WEEKEND – PEOPLE – RANDC

Carmersstraat
Genthof
Spinolarei
Sint-Annarei
Sint-Annakerk
Sint-Walburgakerk
Boomgaardstraat
Hoogstraat
Burg
Predikherenstraat
302
364
110
363
243
222
135
201
195
145
192
150
388
323
376
1
133
143
42
70
130
161

Map 2
HISTORIC CENTRE (SOUTH)

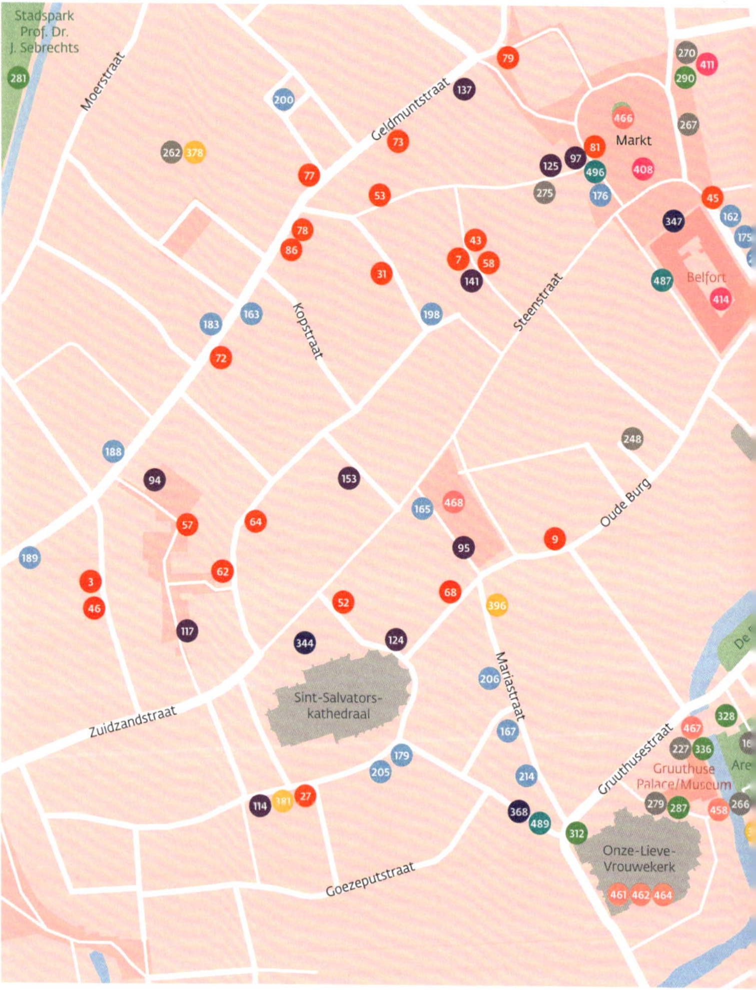

EAT – DRINK – SHOP – BUILDINGS – DISCOVER – CULTURE – SLEEP – WEEKEND – PEOPLE – RANDC

including **ASTRIDPARK QUARTER**

AT – DRINK – SHOP – BUILDINGS – DISCOVER – CULTURE – SLEEP – WEEKEND – PEOPLE – RANDOM

Map 3

NORTH BRUGES

including SINT-GILLIS QUARTER

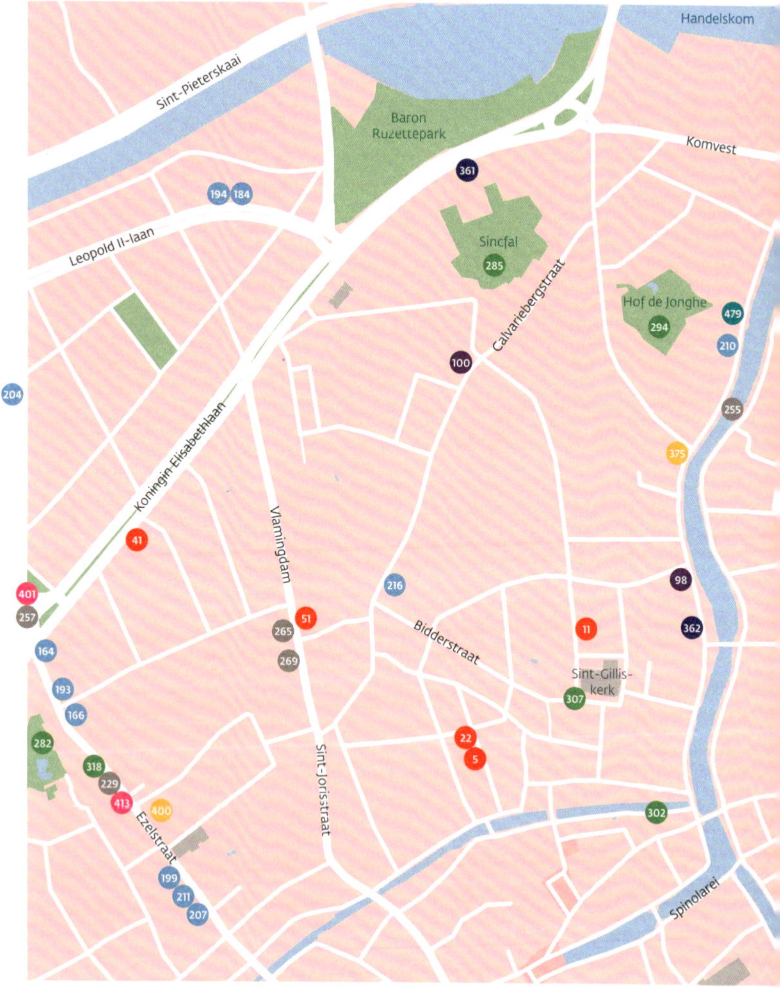

EAT – DRINK – SHOP – BUILDINGS – DISCOVER – CULTURE – SLEEP – WEEKEND – PEOPLE – RANDO

Map 4

EAST BRUGES

including SINT-ANNA QUARTER

– DRINK – SHOP – BUILDINGS – DISCOVER – CULTURE – SLEEP – WEEKEND – PEOPLE – RANDOM

Map 5
SOUTH BRUGES
including BEGIJNHOF QUARTER

EAT – DRINK – SHOP – BUILDINGS – DISCOVER – CULTURE – SLEEP – WEEKEND – PEOPLE – RAND

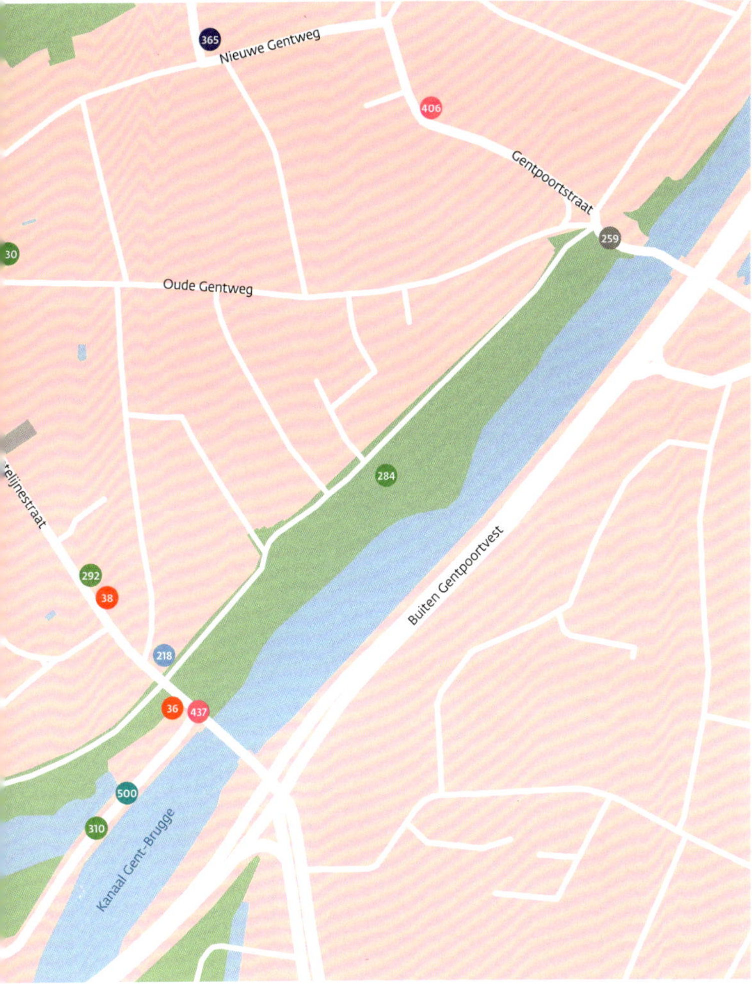

– DRINK – SHOP – BUILDINGS – DISCOVER – CULTURE – SLEEP – WEEKEND – PEOPLE – RANDOM

Map 6

WEST BRUGES

including 'T ZAND QUARTER

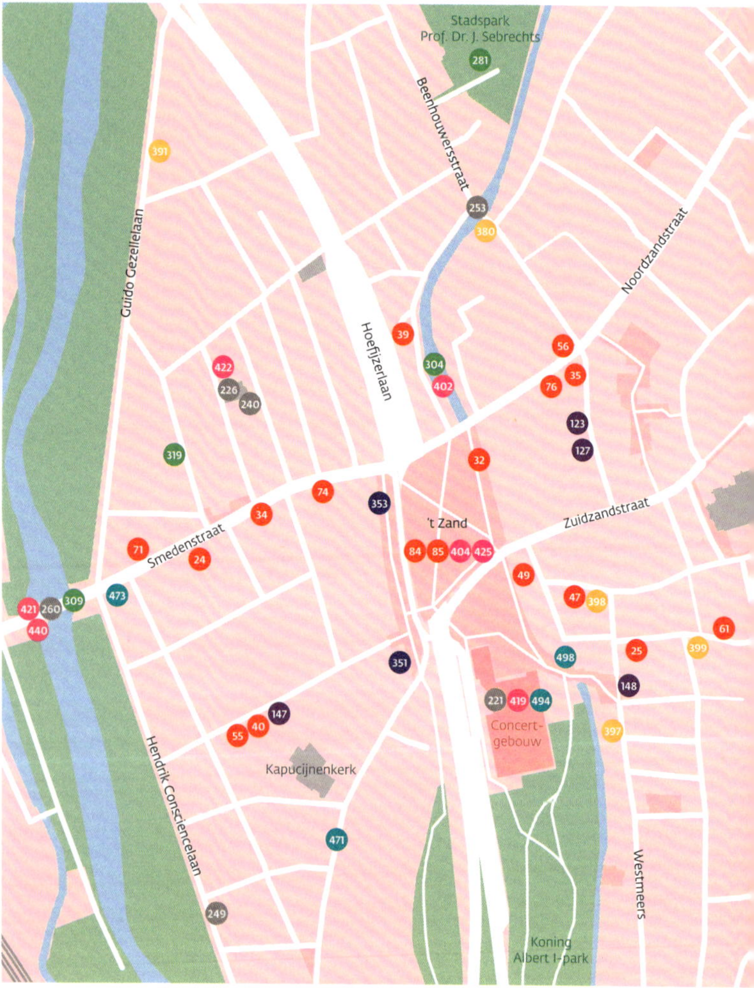

EAT — DRINK — SHOP — BUILDINGS — DISCOVER — CULTURE — SLEEP — WEEKEND — PEOPLE — RANDO

Map 7

SUBURBS

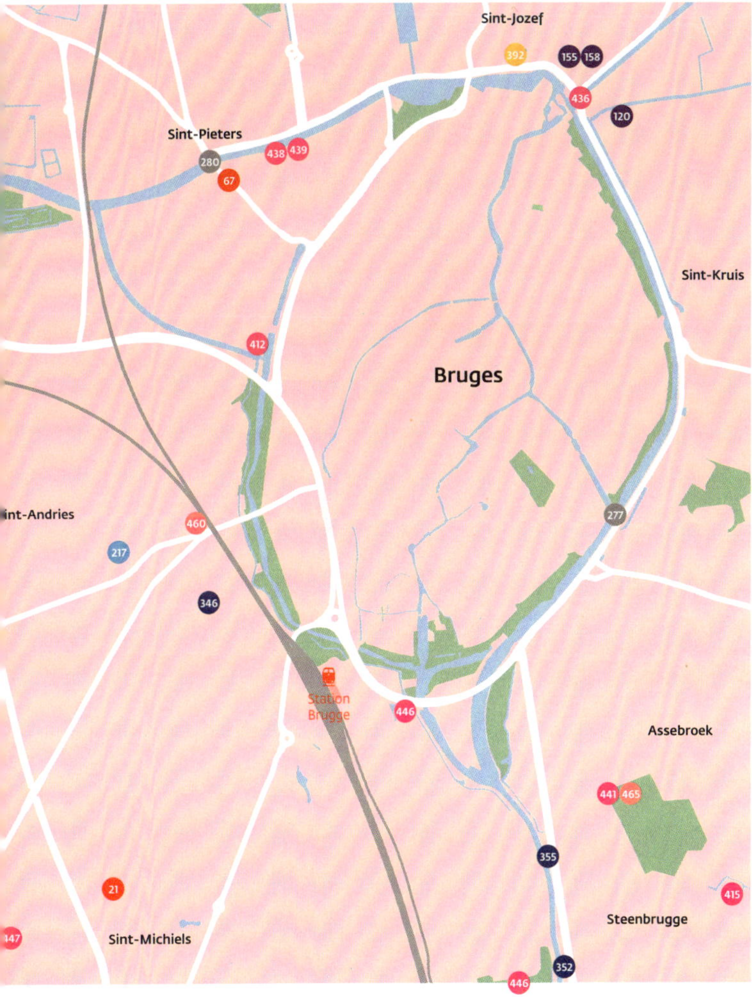

T – DRINK – SHOP – BUILDINGS – DISCOVER – CULTURE – SLEEP – WEEKEND – PEOPLE – RANDOM

Map 8
HINTERLAND

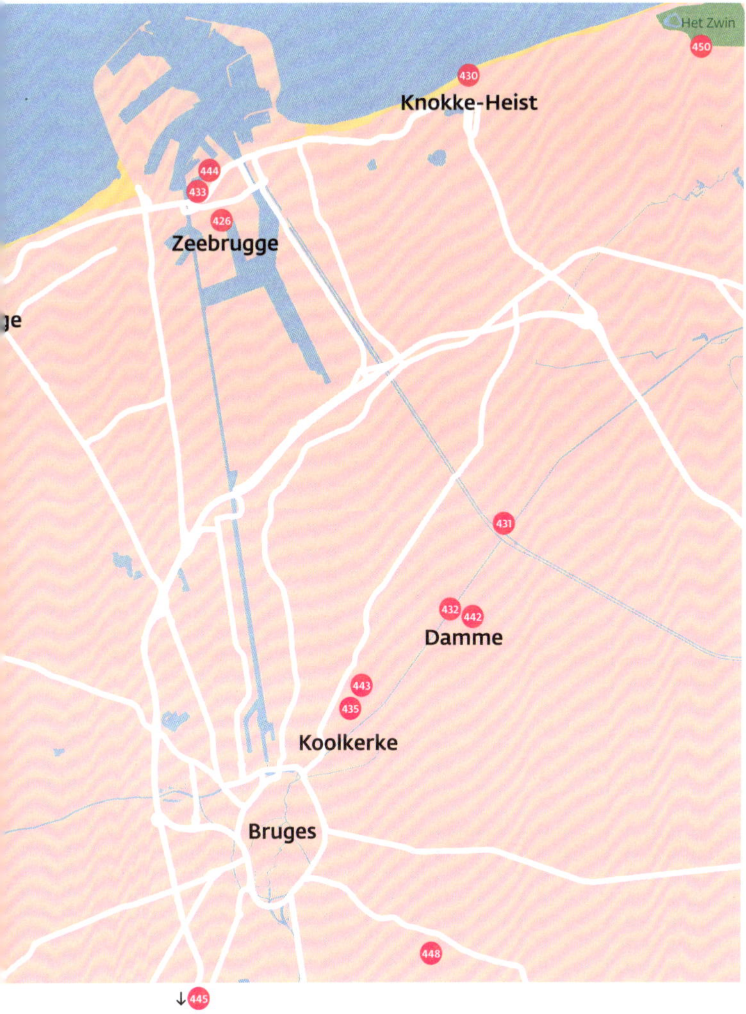
Het Zwin
450
430
Knokke-Heist
444
433
426
Zeebrugge
ge
431
432
442
Damme
443
435
Koolkerke
Bruges
448
↓445

LE PAIN DE SEBASTIEN

DE ZOTTE BAKKER

90 PLACES TO EAT OR BUY GOOD FOOD

The 5 most

CREATIVE RESTAURANTS

1 **LIEVEN**
Philipstockstraat 45
Historic Centre ①
+32 (0)50 68 09 75
etenbijlieven.be

Chef Lieven Vynck brought in interior architect Lieven Musschoot to transform an abandoned corner house in the heart of Bruges. The architect has carefully preserved the old wood beams and marble fireplace of the historic house, but added a wall made from a patchwork of recycled marble strips. Vynck works with his team in a small kitchen at the back where he prepares some miraculous dishes.

2 **BRUUT**
Meestraat 9
Historic Centre ②
+32 (0)50 69 55 09
bistrobruut.be

Bruno Timperman worked in several upmarket restaurants in Bruges before opening a little place of his own in a beautiful spot overlooking an ancient bridge. He works in a basement kitchen just above the water where he creates exceptional dishes using fresh local ingredients.

3 **BONTE B**
Dweersstraat 12
Historic Centre ②
+32 (0)50 34 83 43
restaurantbonteb.be

Bernard Bonte runs a stylish contemporary restaurant with his wife Valerie. The interior was designed to create a relaxed Nordic-inspired space. The kitchen attracts upmarket local diners with its subtle Belgian and French cuisine.

4 **REFTER**
Molenmeers 2
Sint-Anna Quarter ④
+32 (0)50 44 49 00
bistrorefter.com

Bruges chef Geert Van Hecke created this modest bistro behind his acclaimed (but now closed) restaurant De Karmeliet. Designed by local architects noArchitecten, his new place is a bright open space overlooking a formal back garden. The menu includes traditional Flemish dishes like *paling in 't groen* – eel cooked in herbs and garlic.

5 **TOM'S DINER**
West-Gistelhof 23
Sint-Gillis Quarter ③
+32 (0)50 33 33 82
tomsdiner.be

Tom Mestdagh creates innovative dishes in a romantic 16th-century brick house. Located in a quiet neighbourhood, the restaurant attracts a mix of local foodies and adventurous tourists. The ancient interior has been given a modern Scandinavian look with plain wood tables and colourful cushions.

4 REFTER

5 *of the most*
AUTHENTIC BELGIAN
restaurants

6 **'T BAGIENTJE**
Oostmeers 130
Begijnhof Quarter ⑤
+32 (0)50 33 11 20
bagientje.be

It only opened in 2011, but 't Bagientje looks like it has been around for decades. Locals love the retro details like the wood panelling, old clock, porcelain tureens and generous portions. Even the menu comes in the form of a Bruges newspaper from the 1950s, while the cooking draws on old Flemish recipes.

7 **DE STOVE**
Kleine Sint-Amandsstraat 4
Historic Centre ②
+32 (0)50 33 78 35
restaurantdestove.be

This little restaurant in a side street off Markt has been around since 1985. The interior is traditional Flemish style with an iron stove to warm the room in winter. The cooking became a little more inventive after Nico and Chef Debbie took over from the original owners in 2017.

8 BELGIAN PIGEON HOUSE

Sint-Jansplein 12
Historic Centre ①
+32 (0)50 66 16 90
belgianpigeon house.com

This relaxed restaurant located in an old Bruges house is filled with pigeon-racing memorabilia, including framed pictures, old posters and a stained glass window decorated with a pigeon. The hearty cooking is almost all done using a Spanish Josper charcoal oven. The menu includes spicy chicken starter and crisp roast pigeon.

9 DE KOETSE

Oude Burg 31
Historic Centre ②
+32 (0)50 33 76 80
dekoetse-brugge.be

Here is a friendly restaurant in the heart of the old town with an open fire for winter evenings. Located in a 17th-century corner house, De Koetse (the coach) has a simple rustic interior reminiscent of a Flemish country inn. The chef can be counted on to produce the perfect steak, a pot of plump Zeeland mussels or fish grilled on skewers.

10 DILIGENCE

Hoogstraat 5
Historic Centre ②
+32 (0)50 33 16 60
diligence-brugge.be

This is an old Bruges restaurant in a corner house near the main square. The interior is a typical Belgian mix of wood panelling, mirrors and a curved bar. The chef produces traditional Belgian food, with the occasional creative touch. Fans of the film *In Bruges* might recognise the restaurant as the setting for a scene in which the two Irish hitmen meet a prostitute and a dwarf.

5 ROMANTIC RESTAURANTS

11 **'T OUD HANDBOGENHOF**
Baliestraat 6
Sint-Gillis Quarter ③
+32 (0)50 33 19 45

Located in a quiet street near the Sint-Gillis church, this was once a simple local bar where the guild of archers met to drink beer and play billiards. It's now a restaurant run by the owners of a nearby hotel. They have kept the rustic interior, open fire and back courtyard. But they have added a creative menu based on seasonal Belgian specialities like asparagus and mussels, along with authentic local beers.

12 **POMPERLUT**
Minderbroeders-straat 26
Astridpark Quarter ②
+32 (0)50 70 86 26
pomperlut.be

This romantic restaurant occupies a red ochre building from 1612 with a terrace facing the Astridpark. It has a strange interior like a Hobbit house with mushroom ornaments, quirky lamps and an ancient log fire. It was taken over in 2018 by a friendly couple who offer a creative Mediterranean menu based on seasonal produce.

13 DE BOTTELIER

Sint-Jakobsstraat 63
Historic Centre ①
+32 (0)50 33 18 60
debottelier.com

Located next to an old bridge, this small, quirky restaurant is filled with antique clocks, along with vintage lamps, old photographs and a tailor's dummy. You sit at wooden tables in the cluttered interior looking out on a canal. The friendly owner attracts locals and tourists with his affordable lunch menu and careful Belgian cooking. Most days you have to book a table.

14 IN DEN WITTENKOP

Sint-Jakobsstraat 14
Historic Centre ①
+32 (0)50 33 20 59
indenwittenkop.be

An intimate Flemish bistro with red walls, marble table tops and old beer signs. It could almost be Paris, except for the food that comes out of the kitchen. You can order homemade *garnaalkroketten*, eels in cream sauce or a pot of Zeeland mussels served with hand-cut chips.

15 DE SCHAAR

Hooistraat 2
East Bruges ④
+32 (0)50 33 59 79
bistrodeschaar.be

Once an 18th-century inn, this rustic bistro with a waterfront terrace gets its name from the carved stone decorated with scissors on the side wall. The location lies off the beaten track, so it still has a certain local charm. Most of the cooking involves grilled meat and fish cooked by the chef over an open fire.

The 5 best restaurants for

BRUGES ATMOSPHERE

16 **'T GEZELLEKE**
Carmersstraat 15
Sint-Anna Quarter ④
+32 (0)470 12 21 83

This warm neighbourhood bistro lies in a quiet street in the Sint-Anna Quarter. Named after the Bruges poet Guido Gezelle, it's a friendly, romantic place with red checked table cloths, hops hanging from the ceiling and a bust of the poet. The kitchen focuses on Flemish comfort food such as beef stew cooked in Mc Chouffe beer, North Sea fish stew and rabbit simmered in Lindemans cherry beer.

17 **CÉZAR**
Jeruzalemstraat 1
Sint-Anna Quarter ④
+32 (0)50 70 97 84
restaurant-cezar.be

Locals like to eat in this warm, relaxed restaurant near the Jeruzalemkerk (Jerusalem Chapel). The young owners have created a friendly, comfortable spot with decorated wallpaper, low lights and assorted chairs. David is responsible for the imaginative cooking based on old Flemish recipes, while Sarah takes care of the guests.

18 IN 'T NIEUW MUSEUM

Hooistraat 42
East Bruges ④
+32 (0)495 32 62 04
nieuw-museum.com

This friendly family-run restaurant has been around since 1978. It takes its name from a museum that was planned (but never opened) near the restaurant's original location. Now run by Koen and Marijke, it has a cluttered, rustic look, like a Flemish brown cafe, with metal beer signs, old photographs and cooking implements. Most people come here for the massive steaks and hunks of tuna grilled in an ancient brick fireplace.

19 LION BELGE

Langestraat 123
East Bruges ④
+32 (0)496 21 02 44
lionbelge.eu

Sam Foucart has turned an old Bruges bar into an authentic little restaurant where you can eat some of the best Flemish cooking in town. The plain interior still has the original bar, along with small wooden tables and industrial lamps. This is the place to go for a Flemish stew served with a bowl of Belgian chips and a glass of Brugse Zot. The menu for the week is posted on social media.

20 PRO DEO

Langestraat 161
Sint-Anna Quarter ④
+32 (0)50 33 73 55
bistroprodeo.be

A relaxed bistro located in a whitewashed inn from 1562 near the Kruispoort city gate. It has an authentic Bruges atmosphere, like the front room of a favourite aunt, with oak beams, antique furniture and soft jazz playing in the background. The chef favours classic Belgian comfort food like *potjesvlees*, Nieuwpoort shrimp croquettes and Flemish stew.

The 5 best

NEW CONCEPTS

21 **TÊTE PRESSÉE**
Koningin Astridlaan 100
Suburbs ⑦
+32 (0)470 21 26 27
tetepressee.be

Chef Pieter Lonneville has converted an old butcher's shop on the edge of town into a stylish delicatessen with a lunch counter at the back. His aim is to recreate the nostalgic atmosphere of a family meal at a big farmhouse table. He cooks in an open kitchen using fresh local ingredients while incorporating ideas he picked up in Iceland.

22 **NXT DOOR**
West-Gistelhof 21
Sint-Gillis Quarter ③
+32 (0)50 73 79 89
nxtdoor.be

This street food bar opened in 2016 in the house next to Tom's Diner. The interior architect Lieven Musschoot has crafted a striking modern look using raw wood tables, rough brick walls and bright cushions. The kitchen produces tasty bar bites inspired by Asian and South American street food including lamb burger and pulled pork.

23 HUBERT

Langestraat 155-159
Sint-Anna Quarter ④
+32 (0)50 64 10 09
gastrobar-hubert.be

Henk Van Oudenhove has created a relaxed spot for bar food next to his upmarket restaurant Sans Cravate. Named after a local man who formerly lived here, Hubert has been given a hip modern look with bold colours and an open kitchen. The menu on the blackboard changes depending on the season or Henk's latest research, so you might be offered North Sea fish stew or pheasant roasted on the spit.

23 HUBERT

24 TOUGOU

Smedenstraat 47
West Bruges ⑥
+32 (0)50 70 58 02
tougou.be

Jade and Thibault serve innovative food in a stylish lunch spot near the Smedenpoort. The interior has a hip modern look with bare brick, small round tables and a lunch counter. The kitchen uses fresh ingredients to create tasty tapas dishes, including sardines from the small port of Getaria in Spain. Closed in the evening.

25 GOESEPITTE43

Goezeputstraat 43
't Zand Quarter ⑥
+32 (0)50 66 02 23
goesepitte43.be

No problem finding this restaurant. The name is almost the same as the address. It is located in a quiet lane, away from the crowds. The intimate interior has a bright Nordic feel and there is a terrace at the back for summer dining. Chef Jan Supply consistently pleases diners with his creative cooking style based on fresh ingredients.

24 TOUGOU

The 5 best restaurants for

FISH FROM THE NORTH SEA

26 **DEN GOUDEN HARYNCK**
Groeninge 25
Historic Centre ②
+32 (0)50 33 76 37
goudenharynck.be

Hidden down a lane near the Groeninge-museum, this restaurant takes its name from the gilded herring above the door. The chef has been working here for more than 30 years producing creative dishes. He is particularly admired for his innovative fish cooking.

27 **LOBSTER POT**
Sint-Salvators-kerkhof 14
Historic Centre ②
+32 (0)50 66 03 59
lobster-pot.be

This smart, friendly restaurant next to the Cathedral offers fresh seafood straight from the North Sea. The menu includes Zeeland mussels simmered in white wine, bouillabaisse of North Sea fish and lobster *waterzooi*. Or you can splash out on a seafood platter.

30 DEN GOUDEN KARPEL FISHBAR

28 BREYDEL DE CONINC

Breidelstraat 24
Historic Centre ②
+32 (0)50 33 97 46
restaurant-breydel.be

Locals have been coming to this fish restaurant in the heart of Bruges for several decades. They know they will get a decent pot of North Sea mussels simmered in wine, along with perfect chips and delicious mayonnaise. Sometimes they might order a lobster for a special anniversary dinner. Or perhaps they will try the catch of the day for a change. But it will all be perfect.

29 PIETER POURBUS

Pieter Pourbus-straat 1
Historic Centre ①
+32 (0)50 34 11 45
pieterpourbus.com

An attractive restaurant located in a whitewashed corner house dating from 1561. The dining room is a snug place for a winter meal in front of a blazing fire. The menu has a number of fish dishes, including the hearty Flemish fish stew known as *waterzooi*.

30 DEN GOUDEN KARPEL FISHBAR

Huidenvettersplein 4
Historic Centre ②
+32 (0)50 33 34 94
dengoudenkarpel.be

Located in a 17th-century building on the old fish market, Den Gouden Karpel (The Golden Carp) gets its name from the stone carved with a carp above the door. Originally a simple fish stall, it has evolved into a serious fish restaurant, with a fishmonger shop and informal fishbar. Here you can eat fresh fish from Zeebrugge harbour and plump mussels from Zeeland waters.

5 great places for
BRUNCH

31 KOTTEE KAFFEE
Korte Zilverstraat 8
Historic Centre ②
+32 (0)493 53 87 60
kotteekaffee.be

Located down a quiet side street, this hidden coffee house has a trendy interior with a pale wood floor, designer furniture and a long reading table. It's a relaxed spot where locals drop in for a flat white, a special tea or a healthy brunch with seven types of bread, local eggs, two types of ham and homemade jams.

31 KOTTEE KAFFEE

32 NOMAD

't Zand 12
't Zand Quarter ⑥
+32 (0)50 73 64 88
nomadbrugge.be

Margaux and Bram gave up their South African B&B in 2015 to open this hipster kitchen and bar on 't Zand. The kitchen gets most of its supplies from small farms around Bruges, including the owners' own organic farm. The healthy brunch menu features organic juices, a homemade granola mix and veggie burgers.

33 SANSEVERIA

Predikherenstraat 11
Historic Centre ②
+32 (0)50 34 81 43
sanseveria.be

This little brunch cafe occupies a former shop with an old tiled floor and polished wooden counter. The interior is decorated in a retro Flemish style with vintage crockery, a gramophone and those prickly house plants known as sanseveria. The menu lists a range of bagels, along with apple waffles and scones.

34 LE PAIN DE SEBASTIEN

Smedenstraat 31
West Bruges ⑥
+32 (0)50 34 47 44
lepaindesebastien.be

Sebastien Cailliau studied the art of baking bread in France before opening a bakery in Bruges in 2014. He has transformed an old brick house into a hip spot with white walls, industrial lamps and a long breakfast table in the back. His team bake tasty sourdough loaves and authentic baguettes.

35 THAT'S TOAST

Dweersstraat 4
't Zand Quarter ⑥
+32 (0)50 68 82 27

This hip Nordic-style brunch spot is decorated with white walls, spiky plants and bare light bulbs. The kitchen offers an all-day breakfast featuring healthy options like fresh juice, granola, and smoked salmon and avocado on toast. There's also a small walled garden at the back.

The 5 best restaurants for
ASIAN FOOD

36 **HET VISIOEN**
Katelijnestraat 160
South Bruges ⑤
+32 (0)50 73 40 06
hetvisioen.com

This little local restaurant occupies a former cafe with a shady terrace hidden at the back under the trees. It has an old interior with heavy wood furnishings and huge windows that make the place look much larger. The cooking is a mix of classic Belgian dishes along with Indonesian specialities, including grilled tuna steak with lemongrass.

37 **TANUKI**
Oude Gentweg 1
Begijnhof Quarter ⑤
+32 (0)50 34 75 12
tanuki.be

Ivan Verhelle studied the art of cooking in Japan before opening this restaurant. He stands behind the counter preparing traditional sushi and sashimi dishes along with his own creations such as sushi with North Sea grey shrimps. His customers include Japanese tourists looking for a taste of home.

38 **SIVALAI THAI RESTARURANT**

Katelijnestraat 123
South Bruges ⑤
+32 (0)472 32 96 51
sivalai.be

Supong and his wife Atchara opened this Thai restaurant in 2008 in a quiet location away from the crowds. The interior is decorated in a warm, romantic style with wood panelling, low lighting and potted plants. The chef offers authentic Thai cooking, including fried squid and some vegetarian dishes.

39 **CHANG THONG THAI**

Kleine Hoefijzer-straat 1
't Zand Quarter ⑥
+32 (0)50 33 44 05
changthong-thai.be

An intimate Thai restaurant with a warm interior dotted with statues, plants and lamps. The kitchen produces typical Thai cooking including vegetarian dishes.

40 **MIAOW MIAOW**

Hauwerstraat 9
't Zand Quarter ⑥
+32 (0)50 57 08 80
miaow.be

The couple behind this Chinese restaurant create authentic Asian street food including tasty *bing* (sweet pancakes), *gyoza* and sushi. They also have a food truck that goes around Belgian summer festivals.

5 of the best places for
MEDITERRANEAN COOKING

41 **VENTURA**
Koningin Elisabethlaan 48-A
North Bruges ③
+32 (0)50 69 39 74
venturaristorante.be

This modest Italian restaurant is located in the former living room of a Bruges house. The interior is decorated in a sober modern style with an oil painting above the fireplace. The owner is Sicilian while his wife, who does the cooking, is Belgian. She offers authentic Sicilian specialities like *pasta alle sarde*, but also northern Europe dishes such as sour herring in yoghurt sauce.

42 **SUD IN BRUGGE**
Mallebergplaats 5
Historic Centre ①
+32 (0)50 34 45 62
sudinbrugge.com

Luigi Sica's little lunch restaurant and food store is quite discreet. You could easily miss it, yet it is one of the best spots in town for authentic Italian cooking. The owner gets most of his food delivered every Monday from Puglia. He knows where to get hold of the freshest *orecchiette* and the purest olive oil, along with the huge round loaves known as *pane di Altamura*.

43 SALE E PEPE

Kleine Sint-Amandsstraat 1
Historic Centre ②
+32 (0)50 61 51 55

Barbara and Bart run a friendly trattoria with a modern interior in the heart of Bruges. They offer simple, Sicilian home cooking using the best ingredients they can find. Locals come here to eat a simple pizza, *pasta vongole* or *torta di pesche*.

44 QUATRE MAINS

Philipstockstraat 8
Historic Centre ①
+32 (0)50 33 56 50
4mains.com

Chef Olivier Degroote offers original tapas dishes in a relaxed candlelit interior. Locals crowd in after work to share a plate of pigs' cheeks, smoked eel or grilled shrimps. It's often difficult to get a table here.

45 THE OLIVE TREE

Wollestraat 3
Historic Centre ②
+32 (0)50 33 00 81
theolivetree-brugge.com

A friendly Greek restaurant located just a few steps from Markt. The owner offers simple, authentic cooking in a relaxed setting. This is a reliable address for Greek favourites like grilled swordfish and calamari with lemon.

The 5 best restaurants for
CHEAP EATS

46 **GRAN KAFFEE DE PASSAGE**
Dweerstraat 26
Historic Centre ②
+32 (0)50 34 02 32
passagebruges.com

This romantic art deco restaurant has a typical old Bruges interior decorated with mirrors, potted plants and family photographs. The kitchen turns out classic Belgian cooking, including rabbit simmered with plums, Flemish stew, and chips served Belgian style with homemade mayonnaise. Its affordable menu attracts a lively mix of students, locals and tourists.

47 **LOKKEDIZE**
Korte Vulders-
straat 33
't Zand Quarter ⑥
+32 (0)50 33 44 50
bistrolokkedize.be

A brown cafe in a cobbled back street with a romantic interior of brick walls, musical instruments hanging on the walls and a blazing fire in winter. The kitchen serves simple Belgian and Mediterranean cooking at affordable prices.

48 **JILLES**
Braambergstraat 10
Historic Centre ②
+32 (0)50 70 55 55
jilles.be

Jilles D'hulster opened his first burger restaurant in Ghent. It was such a success that he took his concept to Bruges in 2015. The restaurant is a sober Scandinavian-style spot with pale wood tables and a blackboard listing the options. Burgers are paired with Belgian beers.

49 DE MIDDENSTAND

't Zand 20
't Zand Quarter ⑥
+32 (0)50 34 17 50
demiddenstand.com

A friendly Flemish restaurant on 't Zand where locals like to eat. The interior has the crisp, smart look of a traditional French brasserie. The chef pleases regulars with an inexpensive two-course lunch menu based on local cooking. The place quickly fills up on Saturdays when the market is held on the square outside.

50 HUIS DE CLUUSE

Kraanplein 4
Historic Centre ①
+32 (0)474 64 61 09
huisdecluuse.be

This relaxed food bar opened in 2017 in an ancient house dating back to 1270. The interior has been given a modern look with bare brick walls, designer lamps and quirky chairs. You can drop in at lunchtime to choose from an inexpensive tapas menu that includes vegetarian dishes. But it is also a serious beer cafe run by a former barman at 't Brugs Beertje.

48 JILLES

The 5 best places for

REAL BELGIAN CHIPS

51 FRITUUR DE VLAMINGDAM

Vlamingdam 8
Sint-Gillis Quarter ③
+32 (0)50 34 56 78

Gina and Georges Fonteyne run a friendly neighbourhood chip shop decorated in the style of an American roadside diner. It's like a 1950s film set complete with red leatherette seating, neon signs and juke boxes. The owners serve authentic Belgian chips, burgers and Belgian beers.

52 CHEZ VINCENT

Sint-Salvators-kerkhof 1
Historic Centre ②
+32 (0)50 68 43 95
chezvincenet.eu

This is a tiny, friendly chip shop next to the Cathedral where you can order a paper cone of Belgian chips, a salad and a shrimp croquette. But it is small. You can perch downstairs on a bar stool or hunt for an empty table in the little upstairs room.

53 THE POTATO BAR

Sint-Amands-straat 31
Historic Centre ②
+32 (0)50 33 91 19
thepotatobar.be

Two professional chefs launched this hipster chip shop in 2017. The interior has an industrial look with the bar made from potato crates and a long wooden table in the back. They use the best potatoes to make proper Belgian chips, along with inspiring homemade sauces. They also offer tasty *garnaalkroketten*, Belgian pork sausages and Brugse Zot beer.

54 **ROYAL**

Langestraat 181
Sint-Anna Quarter ④
+32 (0)50 68 41 84
frituur-royal.be

This alternative *frituur* serves healthy chips cooked in palm oil for vegetarians and vegans, as well as regular chips fried separately. The menu chalked on a blackboard includes veggie balls and vegetarian burgers, along with healthy juices.

55 **CHARLIE'S CHIPS**

Hauwerstraat 17
't Zand Quarter ⑥
+32 (0)496 41 40 64
charlies-chips-brugge.business.site

A friendly new spot to sit down with a portion of authentic steaming chips. The interior is furnished in a bright, modern style with pink flamingos dotted around to add some colour. The menu also lists hamburgers and homemade Flemish stew.

53 THE POTATO BAR

The 5 best places for a
TASTY SANDWICH

56 **BABETTE**
Noordzandstraat 67
't Zand Quarter ⑥
+32 (0)50 33 00 15
babettebrugge.be

This tiny sandwich shop is squeezed between the fashion stores on Noordzandstraat. The friendly team prepare interesting sandwiches including crab salad, chicken with curry sauce and the Ghent speciality *broodje Martino*. They will also serve you a takeaway coffee or a fresh salad. Try to get here before noon to avoid a long wait.

57 **HAP**
Zilverpand 16
Historic Centre ②
+32 (0)50 61 66 08

A hidden lunch spot in the Zilverpand shopping centre with a long list of sandwiches named after the owner's friends. You can eat sitting at the counter or take away for a picnic in the park. The sandwiches are made on the spot with warm brown rolls straight from the oven. Try the *broodje Alexis* made with Serrano ham, tomatoes, rocket and truffle mayonnaise.

58 DE BELEGDE BOTERHAM

Kleine Sint-Amandsstraat 5
Historic Centre ②
debelegdeboterham.be

Locals like to squeeze into this tiny lunch spot located down a quiet cobbled lane. It occupies a historic house with a wood floor, oak beams and an ancient American bread slicer. Two women work in the back kitchen preparing healthy sandwiches using thin slices of brown bread along with smoked salmon, herring or local ham. They also create salads using the freshest vegetables.

59 BRAZI'S

Sint-Jakobstraat 2
Historic Centre ①
+32 (0)50 49 09 54
brazis.be

Brazilian couple Adenis and Adriana opened this friendly sandwich shop near Markt on a frosty day in 2018. They immediately brought Brazilian warmth to the cold northern streets. They make their sandwiches with small baguettes still warm from the oven. You can order simple crab salad or something more exotic like salted cod. Add a homemade fruit juice and you have the perfect picnic to eat on a canalside bench.

60 SINT-PAULUS

Vlamingstraat 25
Historic Centre ①
+32 (0)50 34 85 70
stpaulus.be

The young staff at Sint-Paulus bakery have to serve customers in three or four languages. But they keep cheerful as they put together sandwiches using authentic baguettes baked every morning in the Bruges suburbs. The sandwich menu lists 21 different fillings including North Sea salad and a classic Ghent-style Martino.

5 *restaurants with* SHADY GARDENS *and* TERRACES

61 **RÉLIVA**
Goezeputstraat 6
't Zand Quarter ⑥
+32 (0)50 33 13 07
reliva.be

Hidden down a quiet cobbled lane, Réliva occupies a 16th-century house with a back garden surrounded by ivy-covered walls. The inventive chef Lien Vandeputte offers a range of meat, fish and vegetarian dishes, listed on the menu under the headings 'farm', 'sea' and 'garden'. Highlights include a North Sea bouillabaisse cooked with herbs straight from the garden.

62 **CAFEDRAAL**
Zilverstraat 38
Historic Centre ②
+32 (0)50 34 08 45
cafedraal.be

This elegant restaurant occupies a 15th-century house with a striking contemporary interior designed in 2011 by Lieven Musschoot. It also has a spacious back garden with a canopy to protect diners when it rains. The cooking is classic French-Belgian style with a few local touches, like fish from the North Sea and beer-flavoured dishes.

63 PARKRESTAURANT

Minderbroeders-straat 1
Astridpark Quarter ②
+32 (0)497 80 18 72
parkrestaurant.be

An elegant restaurant located in a grand mansion facing the Astridpark. The kitchen prepares traditional Belgian cooking using Ardennes beef, fresh salmon and Ostend sole. The garden at the back is the perfect spot for a warm summer evening.

64 PATRICK DEVOS

Zilverstraat 41
Historic Centre ②
+32 (0)50 33 55 66
patrickdevos.be

Patrick Devos runs a restaurant in a late-Gothic house with art nouveau and art deco interiors. You can sit in a wood-panelled dining room, a bright conservatory or outside in the romantic courtyard garden. Devos seeks out produce from the best local farms, and maintains a list of good wines, mainly from French vineyards.

65 ONE

Arsenaalstraat 55
Begijnhof Quarter ⑤
+32 (0)50 33 80 88
one-minnewater.be

Located in a small house near the Minnewater, this restaurant has an intimate dining room with a blazing fire for romantic winter evenings, along with a back garden where you can sit out in the summer. Céline welcomes guests while Pieter cooks traditional Flemish dishes including *garnaalkroketten* and Flemish stew simmered in Chimay beer.

5 *of the best places for* VEGETARIAN *and* VEGAN FOOD

66 **DE PLAATS**
Wapenmakers-straat 5
Historic Centre ①
+32 (0)50 66 03 66
deplaats.be

Graphic artist Frow opened this attractive vegetarian restaurant in 2016. Hidden down a quiet side street, it has three intimate rooms decorated with old floor tiles, school classroom chairs and a large wall photo of a farmer and his dog. The menu lists about 12 vegetarian and vegan dishes, along with Belgian craft beers.

67 **HASHTAG FOOD**
Scheepsdalelaan 37
Suburbs ⑦
+32 (0)50 70 76 70
hashtagfood.be

Dave and Emmanuel have created a cool, friendly spot where local vegans like to eat. Originally located in the centre, they moved in 2017 to an art deco house just outside the old town. The new place has a stylish, Nordic look combined with quirky humour. There's also an automat outside where locals pick up last-minute meals.

66 DE PLAATS

68 LE BÜHNE

Sint-Salvators-koorstraat 6
Historic Centre ②
+32 (0)50 34 66 49

This small restaurant near the Cathedral has just a few tables in a quiet living room where the food is served on vintage crockery. The chef offers inspiring vegetarian options such as vegetable *waterzooi*, but you can also order meat and fish dishes, along with local craft beers.

69 DE BRON

Katelijnestraat 82
Begijnhof Quarter ⑤
+32 (0)50 33 45 26
eethuisdebron.be

Anuschka and Philippe launched Bruges' first vegetarian restaurant more than 25 years ago. It now has a sober Scandinavian interior with black furniture, white walls and a glass roof. Locals come for the tasty seasonal dishes, warm vegetables and healthy grains. You can order as much as you want, from a baby helping to a full plate. It's a popular place and you must book in advance.

70 DE BRUGSCHE TAFEL

Mallebergplaats 7
Historic Centre ①
+32 (0)50 68 39 87
debrugschetafel.be

This intimate place is run by a young couple who have gradually added vegetarian and vegan dishes to their menu. The interior has a warm, rustic feel with wooden shelves, red checked tablecloths and candles in the evening. The chef offers familiar Flemish dishes like Zeeland mussels with chips, along with inspired vegetarian and vegan dishes that take account of food allergies.

The 5 best

FOOD SHOPS

71 **DE OLIJFBOOM**
Smedenstraat 58
't Zand Quarter ⑥
+32 (0)50 34 16 39
deolijfboom.be

Jan Demonie's tiny delicatessen stocks 80 different types of olive oil, along with more than 250 rare herbs and spices. It also has peppers from 35 different regions and hand-rolled M'hamsa couscous from Tunisia. Local chefs come here to buy cooking ingredients they can't find anywhere else in Belgium, such as fresh Japanese *yuzu* and soy sauce smoked over cherry wood.

74 DE KAASBOLLE

72 **DE WESTHOEK**

Noordzandstraat 39
Historic Centre ②
+32 (0)50 33 60 32

This tiny delicatessen is located in a busy shopping street near the Cathedral. Having spent many years working in one of the best restaurants in Bruges, owner Benny Sonneville knows all about cooking. Locals squeeze inside the narrow space to buy specialities like Iberian pata negra ham, local *bloedworst* (blood sausage) and a tasty rough raisin bread.

73 **DIKSMUIDS BOTERHUIS**

Geldmuntstraat 23
Historic Centre ②
+32 (0)50 33 32 43
diksmuidsboterhuis.be

Bruges locals have been coming to this tiny delicatessen since 1933 to stock up on special cheeses and sausages. It's worth entering just to admire the old interior with its brick walls, painted tiles and brass lamps. The owner stocks West Flanders cheeses, Bruges salami and stone-baked breads, along with Spanish tapas.

74 **DE KAASBOLLE**

Smedenstraat 11
't Zand Quarter ⑥
+32 (0)50 33 71 54
dekaasbolle.be

This family-owned shop has been selling speciality cheeses since 1981. It's a friendly place where people come to buy exclusive French cheeses, rare West Flanders varieties and cheese platters for a dinner party.

75 **DELDYCKE**

Wollestraat 23
Historic Centre ②
+32 (0)50 33 43 35
deldycke.be

An upmarket family delicatessen near the Belfry where you can pick up tasty meals to cook in your apartment. The shop also sells Champagne, Belgian caviar and whisky, along with local specialities like Brugse Achten biscuits to take home as a souvenir.

The 5 best places for
ICE CREAM *and* WAFFLES

76 **DE IJSBEER**
Noordzandstraat 73
't Zand Quarter ⑥
+32 (0)50 33 35 34
deijsbeer.be

Sabine and Gino run this Italian ice-cream salon founded back in 1922. It's a bright, friendly place with a selection of 24 flavours made using authentic recipes, along with perfect espresso coffee. It has a few small tables where locals sit with their favourite scoops while old songs play in the background.

76 DE IJSBEER

77 **GELATERIA DA VINCI**

Geldmuntstraat 34
Historic Centre ②
+32 (0)50 33 36 50
davinci-brugge.be

Sylvia launched an authentic Italian gelateria in the heart of Bruges in 1995. She offers more than 40 different flavours including several new creations each season. The staff who work here are the friendliest people in town, even on a busy summer day.

78 **OYYA**

Noordzandstraat 1
Historic Centre ②
+32 (0)50 33 32 13
oyya.be

Mathieu Eyckmans studied at the Gelato University in Italy before opening this smart ice-cream salon. He makes 28 varieties of ice cream fresh every day, including some quite odd creations. He also sells frozen yoghurt and Brussels waffles.

79 **FRED'S**

Eiermarkt 20
Historic Centre ②
fbwic.com

Frederik Van Isacker started selling ice cream in Knokke in 1989 in a shop mysteriously called Australian Home Made Ice Cream. It's now a chain with branches across Europe. His son recently opened a shop in Bruges called Fred's, where he sells 36 different flavours of ice cream made using fresh milk and eggs.

80 **HOUSE OF WAFFLES**

Wollestraat 31
Historic Centre ②
+32 (0)476 27 99 11
thehouseofwaffles.com

The owner of the Torture Museum decided in 2018 to open a waffle restaurant in the building next door. Don't ask why. You can choose a soft rectangular Brussels waffle, or a sweet sticky Liège version. They are freshly made on robust black waffle irons dipping with dough. Customers can then add strawberries, banana, cheese or anything else they fancy.

The 5 best
MARKETS

81 **MARKT**
Markt
Historic Centre ②

Locals come into town on a Wednesday morning to wander around the bustling market on the main square. The stalls sell flowers from West Flanders, local cheeses, potatoes from the polders and meat straight from the farm. It's also a tradition to wait patiently in line at one of the roast chicken vans. From 8 am to 1.30 pm.

82 **VISMARKT**
Vismarkt
Historic Centre ②

Built in 1821, the neoclassical covered fish market is still occupied by local fishmongers who lay out the day's catch on cold stone slabs. You can buy tiny grey shrimps from the Belgian coast and dripping wet North Sea sole landed that morning in Zeebrugge harbour. Held from Tuesday to Saturday, from 8 am to 1.30 pm.

83 DIJVER

84 'T ZAND

83 DIJVER

Dijver
Historic Centre ②

A lively antique market is held along the Dijver waterfront on summer weekends. It attracts local traders who spread out their stuff on wobbly wooden tables under the trees. You might see someone selling old clocks or a stand with an assortment of Catholic statues. Not a food market, but somewhere to pick up an old Belgian waffle iron or a Flemish cookbook.

84 'T ZAND

't Zand
't Zand Quarter ⑥

Locals head on Saturday mornings to 't Zand square to fill their bags with freshly-baked loaves, Belgian cheeses and fish from Zeebrugge. They are often accompanied by small children who snack on free samples and are rewarded at the end of the morning with a warm *boterwafel*. Held on Saturdays from 8 am to 1.30 pm.

85 ZANDFEESTEN

't Zand
't Zand Quarter ⑥
+32 (0)50 44 46 46
visitbruges.be

An enormous flea market sprawls across 't Zand and into the nearby park on three days every summer. Dealers arrive before dawn to set up stands along a five-kilometre route. They come to sell old furniture, Expo 58 souvenirs, bird cages and dusty books. You won't find food stands, but a lot of old cooking equipment, cutlery and wooden speculoos moulds.

5
UNIQUE TASTES
to try before you leave

86 **GORGONZOLA ICE CREAM**
TASTE AT:
oyya
Noordzandstraat 1
Historic Centre ②
+32 (0)50 33 32 13
oyya.be

It sounds strange. But Mathieu Eyckmans won an award for his gorgonzola ice cream with figs and a crumble of caramelised Serrano ham. It was voted the best ice-cream flavour in Belgium in 2018. Try it if you dare at his shop oyya.

87 **MATJES HERRING**
TASTE AT:
Vismarkt
Historic Centre ②

You must try eating raw Matjes Herring while you are in Bruges. It is a delicacy that has sustained the people of the North Sea for centuries. The herring season traditionally begins in mid-June when the first catch is landed. The pickled herring are sold at the fish market on a paper plate with a serving of sliced raw onions and gherkins.

88 BRUGSE ACHTEN

FOUND AT:
Kaashuys Den Hof
Jozef Suvéestraat 6
Astridpark Quarter ②
+32 (0)50 34 57 77
kaashuysdenhof.be

You won't find Brugse Achten in many places. Shaped like a pretzel, these sweet biscuits are handmade according to a 15th-century recipe invented by Mary of Burgundy's cook. The women who work at bakery Oud Huis Deman make limited quantities following the original recipe. They are sold in some local bakeries and delicatessens.

89 BRUGGE OUD

FOUND AT:
Kaashuys Den Hof
Jozef Suvéestraat 6
Astridpark Quarter ②
+32 (0)50 34 57 77
kaashuysdenhof.be

You can try more than 12 local cheeses with Bruges in their name, including a variety called Brugge Dentelle made to look like lace. But most Bruges cheeses are actually made 50 km away in a factory in Moorslede. The one exception is Brugge Oud, a strong hard variety matured for 12 months in the cool cellars of an ancient abbey in the heart of the city. It goes well with a strong Belgian beer like Brugse Tripel or Straffe Hendrik.

90 SPECULOOS

TASTE AT:
Juliette Handmade Biscuits
Wollestraat 31-A
Historic Centre ②
+32 (0)50 34 84 40
juliettes.be

Juliette bakes traditional spicy Belgian speculoos biscuit every morning. You notice the smell of cinnamon as soon as you enter her shop near the Belfry. She creates eight different varieties using traditional recipes, along with other old-style biscuits such as Brugse dentelles.

BRUGES
An Authorised
DEALER
MISS
HERMANUS
UNWIND
HERMANUS
FLY
LOW

HERMANUS

HERMANUS
SIDEBURN
d Gasoline

70 PLACES FOR A DRINK

The 5 most
STUNNING CAFES

91 **CAFÉ VLISSINGHE**
Blekersstraat 2
Sint-Anna Quarter ④
+32 (0)50 34 37 37
cafevlissinghe.be

The oldest bar in Bruges, Café Vlissinghe served its first customers more than five centuries ago. It is a beautiful, historical place with ancient oil paintings, a 16th-century wooden counter and a battered chair possibly owned by the painter Anthony van Dyck. It is full of Flemish atmosphere, especially in winter when regulars sit around the iron stove with their Trappist beers.

92 **ADRIAAN**
Adriaan Willaert-straat 7
Historic Centre ①
coffeebaradriaan.be

This beautiful coffee bar named after the Flemish composer Adriaan Willaert opened in 2017 in a former 19th-century bank facing the city theatre. The neoclassical interior is decorated with pale green walls, old wooden tables and a cabinet filled with coffee-making equipment.

95 LE PAIN QUOTIDIEN

93 DE REPUBLIEK

Sint-Jakobsstraat 36
Historic Centre ①
+32 (0)50 34 02 29
republiekbrugge.be

Attached to the arts cinema, De Republiek is the perfect spot to merge with the local creative crowd. The interior has a rugged airy feel composed of exposed brick walls, industrial lamps and unruly green plants in terrariums. A relaxed spot to park a buggy, eat a healthy lunch and drink a West Flanders beer.

94 VIVA SARA

Zilverpand 7
Historic Centre ②
+32 (0)50 66 76 27
vivasara.be

The Deprez family of Kortrijk launched their Viva Sara concept in Bruges in the summer of 2017. Located on a quiet square in the Zilverpand shopping complex, the new coffee shop is decorated in a striking modern style with a black concrete roof, dark wood furniture and an ancient German coffee roasting machine.

95 LE PAIN QUOTIDIEN

Simon Stevinplein 15
Historic Centre ②
+32 (0)50 34 29 21
lepainquotidien.be

The Le Pain Quotidien bakery and cafe occupies two 19th-century houses with a shared entrance. A long corridor leads to a rambling series of dark rooms furnished with wood floors, carved fireplaces and bookcases. Hidden at the back, you discover a bright conservatory and a walled garden surrounded by old brick houses.

5
AUTHENTIC FLEMISH BARS

96 **HOLLANDSE VISMIJN**
Vismarkt 4
Historic Centre ②
+32 (0)50 33 33 01

The Hollandse Vismijn (Holland Fish Market) is an authentic Bruges bar on the old fish market square. It's a friendly spot where locals like to drink a glass of Brugse Zot while young socialists talk politics in an upstairs room. Drop by on a weekend evening in the summer and you might find an open-air bar, live music and dancing in the street.

96 HOLLANDSE VISMIJN

97 CRAENENBURG

Markt 16
Historic Centre ②
+32 (0)50 33 34 02
craenenburg.be

The Boedt family have run this old-fashioned place for four generations. The cafe is popular with locals who come here to read the newspaper or drink a Belgian beer. The heavy wooden tables, stained-glass windows and gleaming brass chandeliers look ancient. But the building was completely rebuilt in Old Flemish style in 1956.

98 DE REISDUIF

Langerei 30
Sint-Gillis Quarter ③
+32 (0)468 49 39 78

This friendly local cafe feels like a private living room. The snug interior is decorated with a tiled floor, lace curtains and random paintings. You might find yourself squeezed next to a retired politician, a local thriller writer or a chef who has finished work for the day.

99 'T HOF VAN BEROEP

Langestraat 125
Sint-Anna Quarter ④
+32 (0)50 34 83 20
thofvanberoep.com

The Hof van Beroep (Court of Appeal) is a friendly local bar named after the nearby law courts. You may come across the occasional lawyer, but most customers are young locals and students. They come to watch football on big TV screens, eat a generous helping of spaghetti bolognaise and drink a good beer.

100 **DE KALVARIEBERG**
Sint-Clarastraat 163
Sint-Gillis Quarter ③
+32 (0)50 33 67 28
dekalvarieberg.eu

An unpretentious Flemish bar on the edge of town where you can sit among locals with a beer and a simple plate of pasta. It's a comfortable, old-fashioned place, with a billiard table in the back room and a big TV in the corner where they show Club Brugge matches.

97 CRAENENBURG

5 of the most HIDDEN BARS

101 **'T POATERSGAT**
Vlamingstraat 82
Historic Centre ①
+32 (0)495 22 86 50

It's hard to spot the entrance to this vaulted basement bar. During the day, there is nothing to see except a tiny sign with the name 't Poatersgat (The Priest's Hole) taped to a wooden shutter. In the evening, you can descend old stone steps into a large cellar once owned by a church. It attracts a young local crowd with its candlelit atmosphere, good music and long beer list.

102 **COMPTOIR DES ARTS**
Vlamingstraat 53
Historic Centre ①
+32 (0)494 38 79 61
comptoirdesarts.be

Mind your head as you go down the stairs leading to this hidden music bar. The beautiful interior is furnished with wooden tables and candles stuck in bottles. The owner hosts jazz and blues concerts as well as stand-up comedy acts that fill the place on a Monday evening.

103 LE TRAPPISTE BRUGGE

Kuipersstraat 33
Historic Centre ①
+32 (0)475 45 50 66
letrappistebrugge.com

Steep stone steps lead down to an ancient basement bar with 13th-century brick vaulting. It attracts beer fans from all over the world who sit at candlelit tables with a strong drink and a wooden board piled with meat. The menu has a huge choice including rare Trappist beers and a local IPA.

104 ON THE ROCKS

Grauwwerkers-straat 5
Historic Centre ①
+32 (0)50 33 20 37

Locals and students squeeze inside this tiny late night bar located in a narrow mediaeval street. The owner presides over a dark den decorated with mirrors, old record sleeves and orange walls barely touched since the 1970s. A tiny disco at the back lit with dusty disco balls adds to the retro atmosphere. Open from 8 pm until late.

105 DE GARRE

De Garre 1
(off Breidelstraat)
Historic Centre ②
+32 (0)50 34 10 29
degarre.be

It's right in the centre of Bruges, but hidden down a tiny cobbled alley between two chocolate shops, so not everyone knows about this place. It occupies a 16th-century house with bare brick walls and wood beams. The bar has an appealing Bruges atmosphere and offers a choice of 130 different beers.

The 5 most
ROMANTIC BARS

106 **CAFÉ ROSE RED**
Cordoeaniers-straat 16
Historic Centre ①
+32 (0)50 33 90 51
cordoeanier.be

"We're open when we're not closed," it says on the blackboard outside. The interior is decorated with old beer signs and red roses hanging from the ceiling. They stock about 180 different beers, including Sint Bernardus Abt 12 and Saison Dupont. The back garden is a wonderful spot to sit with a summer beer as the sun goes down.

107 **L'ESTAMINET**
Park 5
Astridpark Quarter ②
+32 (0)50 33 09 16
estaminet-brugge.be

This is a comfortable old brown cafe dating from 1900 with hops hanging from wooden beams and jazz music murmuring in the background. Located opposite a small park in a quiet area of Bruges, it is popular with locals and students. The beer list has some interesting brews while the kitchen produces simple bar food.

108 VOLKSCAFÉ SINT-JAKOBS

Sint-Jakobsstraat 60
Historic Centre ①
+32 (0)494 46 61 46

After working for many years in 't Brugs Beertje, Tom Matthys decided in 2015 to create a traditional Flemish *volkscafé*. The interior is furnished with an iron stove, old album covers and faded family photographs. Locals and tourists admire the authentic look, the nostalgic 1960s music and the friendly atmosphere. The beer list includes Roman beer from the oldest brewery in Belgium.

109 DE ZWARTE KAT

Balstraat 43
Sint-Anna Quarter ④
+32 (0)50 44 87 43
visitbruges.be

The Folklore Museum's cafe De Zwarte Kat (The Black Cat) takes its name from a local literary society. You can drink a craft beer in the old interior, stroke the resident black cat and play traditional Flemish pub games like *sjoelbak* in the garden.

110 TERRASTJE

Genthof 45
Historic Centre ①
+32 (0)50 33 09 19

Ian and Patricia run this tiny waterfront cafe which has just six tables inside and another five out on the terrace. Originally from Britain, they have created the perfect Flemish bar with dark wooden furniture, candles and traditional jazz playing quietly in the background. The opening hours listed on a blackboard outside are quirky to say the least.

The 5 best cafes to
CATCH THE SUN

111 **DE WINDMOLEN**
Carmersstraat 135
Sint-Anna Quarter ④
+32 (0)50 33 97 39

Located on a corner near a windmill, De Windmolen is a pleasant place with a dark Flemish interior. It has a small terrace where you can sit next to a lavender plant in a tin pail and an old vine that miraculously produces a few bunches of grapes every autumn.

112 **HOF DE PLEZANCE**

112 HOF DE PLEZANCE

Sint-Jakobsstraat 36
Historic Centre ①
+32 (0)50 34 02 29
republiekbrugge.be

A secret courtyard hidden behind De Republiek is turned into a relaxed summer bar every year. One of the most romantic spots in town, it is enclosed by old brick buildings, including a 15th-century round tower. A makeover in 2018 introduced plant boxes, olive trees and strings of lights, making it the perfect spot to sip a Brugs Tarwebier, a hip cocktail, or a glass of Vinho Verde.

113 PUNTA EST

Predikherenrei 1
Sint-Anna Quarter ④
+32 (0)50 34 94 10
puntaestbrugge.be

This is the place to come in spring and summer to sit on the cobbled waterfront terrace soaking up the sun. The view looking down the Groenerei is particularly romantic as the sun goes down. The kitchen offers homemade lasagne served in blue bowls and the bar serves a good selection of Belgian beers as well as cocktails.

114 MARIE'S HOUSE

Korte Vulders-straat 5
Historic Centre ②
+32 (0)496 74 22 39

Here is a friendly cafe located in an old town house opposite the Cathedral. You can have coffee and cake in an elegant Flemish front room or sit out in the back garden on colourful metal chairs.

115 URB EGG

Various locations
visitbruges.be

Every summer, URB EGG sets up a temporary cafe in an abandoned spot in Bruges. It might be a forgotten garden or a hidden courtyard. The idea is to create an inspiring new urban space where you can drink a Bruges beer in the sun.

The 5 best bars for **JAZZ, BLUES** *and* **INDIE BANDS**

116 **27BFLAT**
Katelijnestraat 27-B
Begijnhof Quarter ⑤
+32 (0)475 97 88 95
27bflat.be

It's easy to miss the entrance to this jazz hideaway on the crowded Katelijnestraat. A new spot in town, it's a relaxed, intimate place with wooden tables, sofas and low lights. Local musicians come here to play jazz and blues on a tiny stage with a grand piano. The shady garden at the back is still something of a local secret.

117 **JOEY'S CAFE**
Zilversteeg 4
Historic Centre ②
+32 (0)50 34 12 64

Stevie has created a relaxed music venue furnished with old tables and assorted chairs. He plays in local band Cajun Moon and so knows the Bruges music scene intimately. Indie bands often drop by to give a blues concert or join an open mike session on Sunday afternoons. The kitchen produces a generous bowl of spaghetti and the bar stocks some interesting beers.

118 'T RISICO

Jeruzalemstraat 53
Sint-Anna Quarter ④
+32 (0)50 49 11 69
trisico.be

This local brown cafe lies in a quiet neighbourhood near the Jeruzalemkerk. It's a typical Flemish place with a tiled floor, wooden furniture and random antiques. The owners offer simple bar food and interesting Belgian beers. Sometimes they will organise an intimate concert featuring moody French chanson or a local blues band. On warm summer nights, you can sit outside in the walled back garden under strings of lights.

119 DE KELK

Langestraat 69
Sint-Anna Quarter ④
+32 (0)487 24 41 03
dekelk.be

This laidback music bar is one of those hidden Bruges spots most tourists never find. Located on the trendy Langestraat, it has been around since 1909. When the young couple Vincent De Jaegher and Lisa Demeyere took over in 2017, they redecorated the walls with vintage wallpaper and turned the back room into an intimate performance space.

120 IN'T VRIJE

Zuidervaartje 3
Suburbs ⑦
+32 (0)485 62 51 72

Located next to a football pitch just outside the Dampoort, this sports bar attracts a young crowd. It's a relaxed spot away from the crowds where you can pick up a Belgian beer, order a plate of paella and maybe catch a concert by a local band.

The 5 coolest

COCKTAIL BARS

121 **BRUGSE GIN CLUB**
Jozef Suvéestraat 19
Astridpark Quarter ②
+32 (0)472 62 82 43
brugseginclub.be

Knock on the door to enter Edward Vanhoutte's intimate gin bar. Hidden down a quiet lane, the room holds no more than 20 people, so you may be turned away on a busy night. Vanhoutte has built up an exceptional collection of almost 400 different gins including some rare bottles.

122 **GROOT VLAENDEREN**
Vlamingstraat 94
Historic Centre ①
+32 (0)50 68 43 56
grootvlaenderen.be

A serious cocktail bar located in an impressive baroque town house with a dark wood interior. The friendly bartenders know how to shake a Long Island Iced Tea or a Bloody Mary. They also serve interesting Belgian beers.

123 **GIN & WHISKY LOUNGE**
Dweersstraat 22
't Zand Quarter ⑥
+32 (0)474 91 25 35
ginandwhiskyshop.be

Located in an old brick gabled house, this relaxed spot opened in 2018. It offers a range of exclusive gins and whiskies, along with tapas. You can sit in the lounge or out in the walled courtyard at the back.

125 **BAR'N**

124 LA CASITA

Sint-Salvators-kerkhof 5
Historic Centre ②
+32 (0)494 23 99 11

This tiny bar hidden behind the Cathedral has a few tables outside squeezed next to Sint-Salvators ancient walls. The friendly young owner Nina Corty keeps interesting beers including Sint-Bernardus on tap. She also offers classic cocktails and tapas dishes.

125 BAR'N

Sint-Amandsstraat 2
Historic Centre ②
+32 (0)468 22 48 85

Gaëlle Boedt opened her little cocktail bar in 2015 behind cafe Craenenburg, an old Bruges bar run by her father. The two places couldn't be more different. The cocktail bar has a dark, romantic interior created by Frederiek Van Pamel with Moroccan tiles, candles and a cow skull. Locals come here for the friendly mood and the gin cocktails flavoured with fresh herbs and spices.

5 cosy
COFFEE BARS

126 **CAFUNÉ**
Academiestraat 8
Historic Centre ①
+32 (0)484 97 65 61
cafune.be

This little coffee shop has brought a cool Scandinavian look to Bruges with its bare brick, ancient oak beams and cool indie music. It's a friendly, relaxed spot where the barista makes his coffee on a La Marzocco machine using beans from several independent roasters.

127 **LI O LAIT**
Dweersstraat 30
't Zand Quarter ⑥
+32 (0)50 70 85 70
liolait.be

Li Vandamme and Lieven Verstraete have created a relaxed coffee bar in an old Bruges house where the Belgian artist Roger Gobron once lived. The coffee bar occupies the three downstairs rooms, where you still see traces of the former occupants including old wallpaper. There is also an intimate courtyard at the back with two benches where you can sit out in the sun.

126 **CAFUNÉ**

128 I LOVE COFFEE

Sint-Jakobsstraat 10
Historic Centre ①
+32 (0)498 51 63 40
ilovecoffee.be

Koenraad Desmet roasts his own beans to create some unique coffees. The dark, rugged cafe interior has a tiled floor and bare brick walls. Sacks of coffee beans left lying around add to the industrial look. You can perch inside at a small table or take your coffee out to the terrace at the back.

129 VERO CAFFÈ

Sint-Jansplein 9
Historic Centre ①
+32 (0)50 70 96 09

Chloë Kremar opened this relaxed coffee bar in 2014 where she serves good coffee along with tasty lemon muffins. The interior is decorated in modern style with bare whitewashed walls and potted plants. On summer days you can sit out on the pavement at a white metal table or squeeze into the tiny walled courtyard at the back.

130 BRAZILA

Mallebergplaats 1
Historic Centre ①
+32 (0)50 33 09 29
brazila.be

Barista Mike runs a serious coffee bar in a quiet corner of town. The coffee comes from Brazila's own roastery using beans from Brazil and Guatemala. Mike also offers rare wild *kopi luwak* coffee made with civet cat excrement, as well a huge stock of teas in labelled tins, ranging from Yorkshire Gold to Jasmine Pearl.

The 5 most

UNUSUAL CAFES

131 **BOOKS & BRUNCH**
Garenmarkt 30
Astridpark Quarter ②
+32 (0)50 70 90 79
booksandbrunch.be

Tabitha Ackaert and Jos Deroo have created a relaxed secondhand bookstore where they also serve healthy food and good coffee. You find thousands of books on pale green shelves, including an assortment of English books in an upstairs room. The owners have also created a little playroom for kids at the back with cute toadstool chairs.

132 **HERMANUS**
Langestraat 53
Sint-Anna Quarter ④
+32 (0)50 73 83 73
hermanusbruges.be

One of the coolest spots in Bruges, Hermanus was originally a cluttered shop filled with motorcycles, engine parts and biker gear. The owners, Andy and Evy, added a cafe with exposed brick walls, vintage chairs and old motorcycle photos. And then in the winter of 2018 they moved to a larger location in the suburbs. But they have kept the relaxed mood of their 'caffeine and gasoline store'.

133 EXCELLER BIKES

Philipstockstraat 43
Historic Centre ①
+32 (0)50 70 68 12
excellerbikes.com

A specialised bike shop in the centre of Bruges where you can order a customised bike or get a quick repair done to a Brompton folding bike. The store also sells distinctive Belgian cycling jerseys, Brooks saddles and hip bike accessories. You can also drop in for a coffee served with a bowl of biscuits, or sit outside at a little round table with a craft beer from Brussels Beer Project.

134 YESTERDAY'S WORLD

Wijngaardstraat 6
Begijnhof Quarter ⑤
+32 (0)476 45 85 42

A cramped little bar with a list of 65 bottled beers on the menu along with tapas to nibble. But it is also an antique shop where you can buy the little round table where you are seated, or pick up an antique ornament to take home. Look out for occasional concerts in this space.

135 LUCIFERNUM

Twijnstraat 6
Historic Centre ①
lucifernum.be

The eccentric Willy Retsin has furnished a crumbling former Masonic Lodge with a bizarre collection of symbolist paintings, dusty books and quirky statues. He opens it on Sunday evenings to allow guests to wander through the cluttered rooms, spill out into the overgrown garden and drink a rum cocktail.

5 stylish spots for AFTERNOON TEA

136 **THE GULLIVER TREE**
Cordoeaniersstraat 4
Historic Centre ①
+32 (0)50 73 15 16
thegullivertree.be

Two sisters, Janey and Jilly, established this cool little cafe in a former stationery shop in 2014. Located down a quiet lane, it has white walls, spiky house plants and quiet indie music. The friendly young team will bring you a perfect flat white coffee, or an Earl Grey tea.

137 **DE MEDICI SORBETIÈRE**
Geldmuntstraat 9
Historic Centre ②
+32 (0)50 33 93 41
demedici.be

Jurgen and Siska run an elegant tea room behind a gorgeous blue art nouveau façade. Despite the busy location, they have created a quiet, relaxed place with a romantic upstairs room and a walled terrace at the back. The tea is served on a tray with a scoop of homemade sorbet, a Dumon chocolate and a bowl of cream.

138 **HOTEL DE ORANGERIE**
Kartuizerinnen-straat 10
Historic Centre ②
+32 (0)50 34 16 49
hotelorangerie.be

Hotel de Orangerie offers afternoon tea in an intimate dining room or outside on a waterfront terrace. You are brought sandwiches, scones with clotted cream and Belgian patisserie, along with a choice of eleven types of tea. Everything is prepared in the morning using ingredients supplied by local shops.

139 DE PROEVERIE

Katelijnestraat 6
Begijnhof Quarter ⑤
+32 (0)50 33 08 87
deproeverie.be

De Proeverie is an old-fashioned tearoom with several little rooms decorated in the style of 18th-century salons. The coffee is served on a small oval tray along with a saucer of cream and a plate of four handmade chocolates from the family shop across the street.

140 SCOTTISH LOUNGE

Peperstraat 3
Sint-Anna Quarter ④
+32 (0)50 33 88 83
adornes.org

The Adornes family have links with Scotland dating back to the 15th century. The story is told in a museum next to the Jeruzalemkerk and echoed in the Scottish Lounge they created in 2018. Furnished with leather sofas, polished tables and art books, the lounge could be a room in a Scottish castle. Here you can serve yourself with tea and Scottish shortbread. You just leave the money in a jar.

140 SCOTTISH LOUNGE

The 5 best

WINE BARS

141 **BAR JUS**

Kleine Sint-Amands-straat 10
Historic Centre ②
+32 (0)50 61 32 77

This little wine shop opened in 2014 in a contemporary interior near the main square. It doesn't offer much more than a couple of tables and a few bar stools, but it's a relaxed place to stop for a glass of Portuguese wine or a special gin. The food consists of wooden boards laden with cold meats or interesting cheeses. Closed at weekends.

142 **BLEND**

Kuipersstraat 6-8
Historic Centre ①
+32 (0)497 17 20 85
uncorked.be

Two local wine sellers with vineyards in Tuscany have transformed an old shop in the centre into a stylish wine bar. The interior is decorated with pale wood furniture, designer lamps and big windows looking out on the street. The owners, both voted Belgian Sommelier of the Year in the past, offer 30 different wines by the glass.

142 BLEND

143 CUVEE

Philipstockstraat 41
Historic Centre ①
+32 (0)50 33 33 28
cuvee.be

This relaxed wine bar is a good spot to try out organic wines from small French and Italian vineyards. Located at the back of a wine shop, the intimate space is furnished with 1950s vintage chairs and low tables. The bar offers about 15 wines served by the glass, along with tapas.

144 TAPASBAR EST

Braambergstraat 7
Historic Centre ②
+32 (0)478 45 05 55

This intimate wine bar is located in a 17th-century brick building once occupied by the corn merchants' guild. The owners serve uncommon wines along with plates of South American tapas. They also organise French chanson and blues concerts on Sunday nights in the romantic interior.

145 RIESLING & PINOT

Hoogstraat 33
Historic Centre ①
+32 (0)50 84 23 97
riesling-pinot.be

Wine expert Casimir Dusart has created a stylish wine bar where he offers a selection of German wines. The interior has a warm, casual look with old oak beams, small round tables, and little candles. He has 40 different wines in stock, including 15 to sample in the bar.

The 5 best bars for
LATE NIGHTS

146 **DE COULISSEN**
Jakob van Ooststraat 4
Historic Centre ①
decoulissen.be

Hidden inside a grey neoclassical building once occupied by a bank, De Coulissen is a good spot to begin the night. The old interior was recently given a cool makeover by designer Will Erens of Puresang agency to create a trendy lounge bar and stylish dance floor lit by LED lamps.

147 **DE VETTEN OS**
Hauwerstraat 5
't Zand Quarter ⑥
www.vettenos.be

Established in 1887, this ancient brown cafe near 't Zand was renovated in 2018. The cool young owners offer homemade spaghetti, live concerts and tips on where to find the best bands in town.

148 **THE VINTAGE**
Westmeers 13
't Zand Quarter ⑥
+32 (0)50 66 67 80

A relaxed spot close to the Concertgebouw where you can sit out on the terrace in the summer to catch the late evening sun. Locals come here for the long beer list, homemade spaghetti and regular live concerts. The bar has no less than eight beers on tap including La Chouffe and dark red Rodenbach from West Flanders.

149 'T VERDRIET VAN BELGIË

Sint-Jansstraat 1
Historic Centre ①
+32 (0)498 61 74 58

Local students mingle with tourists in this relaxed bar in the centre of Bruges. It is a simple modern place with a limited range of beers and an even more limited range of food. But it's a friendly place to listen to cool tracks and the occasional live concert.

150 CHARLIE ROCKETS

Hoogstraat 19
Historic Centre ①
+32 (0)50 33 06 60
charlierockets.com

It used to be the oldest cinema in Bruges. Now it's a youth hostel with a lively bar where backpackers exchange travel tips. The interior is decorated like an American roadside bar with neon signs, a pool table, movie posters and rock memorabilia. A good spot to catch a live concert by a local band.

5 *great stops on a* BEER TOUR *of Bruges*

151 **DE HALVE MAAN BREWERY**
Walplein 26
Begijnhof Quarter ⑤
+32 (0)50 44 42 22
halvemaan.be

The last family brewery in Bruges, De Halve Maan brews Brugse Zot and the strong Staffe Hendrik. In 2016 the brewery built a 3-km underground pipeline to carry beer to its bottling plant outside the town. It's worth taking a brewery tour to discover the brewing process and step out onto the roof terrace for an unexpected view of the old town.

152 **BOURGOGNE DES FLANDRES BREWERY**
Kartuizerinnen-straat 6
Historic Centre ②
+32 (0)50 33 54 26
bourgogne desflandres.be

This tiny brewery is hidden away in a dark attic in the heart of Bruges. Here the Belgian brewer Anthony Martin has lovingly revived the sour dark red Bruges ale Bourgogne des Flandres, originally launched in 1909. The audio tour takes you up into the tiny brewery where you can smell the malt and listen to the brewer tell his story, ending with a tasting session in a canalside bar.

152 BOURGOGNE DES FLANDRES BREWERY

153 'T BRUGS BEERTJE

Kemelstraat 5
Historic Centre ②
+32 (0)50 33 96 16
brugsbeertje.be

You no longer find Daisy behind the bar or Jan delivering a beer seminar in the back room. Founded in 1983, this mellow Flemish bar has been taken over by a young team, but the spirit of the place has survived. The dark interior is decorated with old beer signs and hop plants hanging from the ceiling. You will find about 300 beers in stock at any time as well as rare seasonal brews.

154 'T BRUGSCH BIERATELIER

Wijngaardstraat 13
Begijnhof Quarter ⑤
+32 (0)478 33 49 69
brugschbieratelier.be

This tiny bar near the Begijnhof looks strange inside, with dusty banknotes hanging from the ceiling and beer mats attached to the walls. But it is a serious place for beer. The owner offers a tasting menu of 12 different Belgian beers served in small glasses on a long wooden tray.

155 FORT LAPIN BREWERY

Koolkerkse Steenweg 32
Suburbs ⑦
+32 (0)495 50 26 70
fortlapin.com

Kristof Vandenbussche launched his craft brewery Fort Lapin in 2011. The friendly owner takes visitors around the modern brewing rooms on Saturdays. At the end of the tour you can sample his Fort Lapin 8 and other more rare beers in a charming tasting room decorated with vintage furniture and 1970s wallpaper.

The 5 best

BRUGES BEERS

to try

156 **BRUGSE ZOT BLOND**
AT: CAMBRINUS
Philipstockstraat 19
Historic Centre ①
+32 (0)50 33 23 28
cambrinus.eu

This lovely local beer is brewed at De Halve Maan with a mix of four varieties of malt and two types of hop. The name recalls an incident in the Middle Ages when Emperor Maximilian joked that Bruges was full of *zotten*, or mad people.

157 **STRAFFE HENDRIK TRIPEL**
AT: DE HALVE MAAN BREWERY
Walplein 26
Begijnhof Quarter ⑤
+32 (0)50 44 42 22
halvemaan.be

The last authentic *Brugs tripel bier* (Tripel beer from Bruges), Straffe Hendrik was specially brewed in 1981 to celebrate the unveiling of a statue dedicated to the patron saint of brewers. You can taste this strong, golden beer in the brewery's cobbled yard.

158 **FORT LAPIN TRIPEL 8**
AT: FORT LAPIN BREWERY
Koolkerkse Steenweg 32
Suburbs ⑦
+32 (0)495 50 26 70
fortlapin.com

The small Fort Lapin brewery has slowly expanded its range since it started brewing in 2011. It now has at least eight beers to try including the original Fort Lapin Tripel 8.

159 **DEN BRUINEN OS**
AT: BOURGOGNE DES FLANDRES BREWERY
Kartuizerinnen-straat 6
Historic Centre ②
+32 (0)50 33 54 26
bourgogne desflandres.be

The Belgian brewer Anthony Martin creates interesting old ales in the heart of Bruges. His headline beer Bourgogne des Flandres is a fruity, reddish beer. But he also brews a malty brown ale called Den Bruinen Os, along with occasional experiments.

160 **TRIPEL DE GARRE**
AT: DE GARRE
De Garre 1
(off Breidelstraat)
Historic Centre ②
+32 (0)50 34 10 29
degarre.be

A sweet ale with a firm head brewed for the Staminee De Garre. It is brewed by Brouwerij Van Steenberge, but only sold on tap in one hidden bar in Bruges.

'T APOSTELIENTJE

60 PLACES TO SHOP

5 *exceptional*
SHOP INTERIORS

161 **ROMBAUX**
Mallebergplaats 13
Historic Centre ①
+32 (0)50 33 25 75
rombaux.be

This gorgeous family business is a reminder of the days before the internet killed off the music store. It is worth entering just to wander through the labyrinth of small rooms with their original mosaic floors, stained glass and wood panelling. Run by the same family for three generations, it is crammed with every imaginable music genre, from rare classical composers to new Flemish folk.

162 **APOTHEEK DRYEPONDT**
Wollestraat 7
Historic Centre ②
+32 (0)50 33 64 74

Even a mild headache gives you an excuse to enter this beautiful pharmacy founded by Doctor Dryepondt. It might look like a museum, but it is an authentic chemist's dating back to 1835. It's worth stepping inside just to admire the tiled floor, wooden counters and rows of brown medicine jars.

163 SCOTCH & SODA

Noordzandstraat 21
Historic Centre ②
+32 (0)50 89 09 11
scotch-soda.com

The fashion chain Scotch & Soda occupies the gorgeous art nouveau lobby of the Grand Hotel du Sablon. The store took over the space in 2011, but carefully preserved the marble fireplaces, antique lift and wood panelling from 1908. They even kept the original hotel sign on the front of the building.

164 CHAPELLERIE BAECKELANDT

Ezelstraat 120
North Bruges ③
+32 (0)472 30 62 33
hoedenbrugge.be

Located in a corner building near the Ezelpoort, this is where local women come to buy a hat for a wedding while men might try on a Panama Hat for the beach. Frédérique Baeckelandt displays her creations in a beautiful old interior with a tiled floor and oak beams. She will also design a unique hat for special occasions.

165 THE CHOCOLATE LINE

Simon Stevinplein 19
Historic Centre ②
+32 (0)50 34 10 90
thechocolateline.be

Dominique Persoone sells outstanding chocolates in a 15th-century house once owned by a wine merchant. The former chef works together with food scientists to create chocolates flavoured with odd ingredients like fried onions, salty bacon and tobacco leaves. The shop was redesigned in 2016 to include an open workshop and a small chocolate museum.

The 5 best local
CHOCOLATE SHOPS

166 **SPEGELAERE**
Ezelstraat 92
Sint-Gillis Quarter ③
+32 (0)50 33 60 52
chocolaterie spegelaere.be

Established in 1954, this is the oldest chocolate shop in Bruges. It stands on a quiet street away from the tourist crowds, so customers are mainly locals. They come for the authentic chocolates including the house speciality *Brugse Kasseien* made in the shape of the local cobblestones.

167 **DEPLA**
Mariastraat 20
Historic Centre ②
+32 (0)50 34 74 12
poldepla.be

Based in a workshop founded by his father in 1958, Pol Depla creates handmade chocolates using the best cocoa beans from ethical growers. He sometimes boosts the flavour by adding unexpected ingredients like flower petals. The chocolates are sold in a sleek modern shop near the Sint-Janshospitaal.

168 **SWEERTVAEGHER**
Philipstockstraat 29
Historic Centre ①
+32 (0)50 33 83 67
sweertvaegher.be

This little shop lies off the tourist trail in a quiet street behind Markt. It's run by a West Flanders family that has been in the chocolate business since 1933. They use the best chocolate to create special filled pralines with chic names like Grenoble and Snobinet.

169 **DUMON**
Eiermarkt 6
Historic Centre ①
+32 (0)50 34 62 82
chocolatierdumon.be

Stephan Dumon began creating delicious handmade pralines in his garage in 1992. He now makes his chocolates in a workshop in Torhout and sells them in a tiny shop near Markt and in a new store on Simon Stevinplein.

170 **SUKERBUYC**
Katelijnestraat 5
Begijnhof Quarter ⑤
+32 (0)50 33 08 67
sukerbuyc.be

The Depreter family started creating handmade chocolates in a room behind their shop in 1977. They now employ a young chef who comes up with new recipes, as well as unusual chocolate souvenirs. Here is the place to come for a chocolate jigsaw puzzle or an edible chocolate box.

167 **DEPLA**

The 5 best shops for WINE *and* BEER

171 **DE BIERBOOM**
Langestraat 73
Sint-Anna Quarter ④
+32 (0)50 34 99 36
debierboom.be

It's a bit of a hike from the centre, but this friendly beer store is a hidden delight. Owner Rudy Vossen stocks a limited selection of rare Belgian beers including the exclusive Westvleteren Tripel. It has a few simple tables in the back room where enthusiasts from far-off countries gather to sample eclectic beers from small breweries, including Rudy's own Bierboom brews.

172 **FEYS-VAN ACKER**
Raamstraat 1 bis
Historic Centre ①
+32 (0)50 33 21 98
feys-vanacker.be

One of the oldest wine dealers in Belgium, Feys-Van Acker have been bringing distinctive French wines to Bruges since 1822. The business moved in 1966 to the cellars of an old brewery used as an air raid shelter in the Second World War. The owners store about 500 different wines in these chilly vaults.

173 STRUISE BEERSHOP

Burg 15-2
Historic Centre ②
+32 (0)495 28 86 23
struise.com

De Struise Brouwers (brewers) create distinctive craft beers in an old schoolhouse in the village of Oost-vleteren. They sell them in a little shop next to the Holy Blood Basilica in Bruges on Thursdays, Fridays and Saturdays. You can pick up unique award-winning brews with curious names such as Pannepot, Tsjeeses or the ridiculously strong Black Damnation V.

174 BACCHUS CORNELIUS

Academiestraat 17
Historic Centre ①
+32 (0)50 34 53 38
bacchuscornelius.com

This rambling beer shop is a bit like a dusty museum. It's run by a friendly young woman who stocks about 450 different beers. You come across rare brews you can't find anywhere else, like De Dolle Dulle Teve (mad bitch), De Dochter van de Korenaar beers and Cornelius' own house beer.

175 THE BOTTLE SHOP

Wollestraat 13
Historic Centre ②
+32 (0)50 34 99 80
thebottleshop.be

This specialised beer shop in the heart of Bruges stocks over 600 different bottled beers. The friendly staff can explain the different beers they have in stock and maybe dig out something unusual from the cellar to match your taste. They have some rare brews including a beer called The Pineapple One brewed exclusively for the shop by Fort Lapin brewery.

5 of the best
BOOKSHOPS

176 DE REYGHERE

Markt 12
Historic Centre ②
+32 (0)50 33 34 03
dereyghere.be

The oldest bookshop in Flanders, De Reyghere (The Heron) was founded by Edmond De Reyghere in 1888. Located on the main square, it sells Dutch novels as well as international newspapers, magazines and foreign fiction. A second shop next door is devoted to maps, dictionaries and travel guides. In 2013, the bookshop marked its 125th anniversary by turning the family living room above the shop into a literary salon.

177 RAAKLIJN

Kuipersstraat 1
Historic Centre ①
+32 (0)50 33 67 20
raaklijn.be

Jean Dhartet founded this serious literary bookshop back in 1961 when Bruges was still a sleepy backwater. After several moves, he is now settled in a handsome building with old wood floors and white walls next to the public library. He stocks the best Dutch fiction, along with books on architecture, art and philosophy.

176 **DE REYGHERE**

178 BRUGSE BOEKHANDEL

Dijver 2
Historic Centre ②
+32 (0)50 33 29 52
brugseboekhandel.be

This traditional family-run bookshop was established in 1934 in a gabled building on the Dijver waterfront. Known to locals as De Meester, it's a rather old-fashioned place with a wide range of books on lace as well as a large section devoted to Bruges art and history.

179 MARC VAN DE WIELE

Sint-Salvators-kerkhof 7
Historic Centre ②
+32 (0)50 33 63 17
marcvandewiele.com

Located in a white corner building behind the Cathedral, Marc Van de Wiele's antiquarian store draws book lovers from all over the world. Founded back in 1976, it stocks beautiful leather-bound atlases, rare art books and obscure studies of witchcraft. Auctions are held twice a year.

180 DEN ELDER

Langestraat 84
Sint-Anna Quarter ④
+32 (0)50 34 18 29
denelder.be

Locals love to search the shelves of this small secondhand bookstore for unexpected finds. The owner also stocks old vinyl records, CDs and classic films on video. Most of the books are in Dutch, but you might stumble upon a forgotten art book or novel in English.

5 hip addresses for FASHION

181 **RUTH**
Sint-Jakobsstraat 55
Historic Centre ①
+32 (0)50 69 88 99
boetiekruth.be

Ruth Niville has created a unique women's fashion store in a beautiful 1908 corner building near the Sint-Jakobskerk. The interior was redesigned in 2015 by Ghent architect collective Urbain to create a shop on two floors that feels more like cool Amsterdam than cosy Bruges. Ruth fills the racks with her personal pick of clothes by creative designers like Sessùn, Humanoid and Momoni.

181 RUTH

182 TWEE MEISJES

Sint-Jakobsstraat 61
Historic Centre ①
+32 (0)50 33 16 61
tweemeisjes.be

This little boutique takes its name from a Flemish folk song by Flemish singer-songwriter Raymond van het Groenewoud about two girls reading fashion magazines on the beach. Owner Margriet has created a relaxed, summery mood in her shop, with each item of clothing given the name of a song.

183 L'HÉROINE

Noordzandstraat 32
Historic Centre ②
+32 (0)50 33 56 57
lheroine.be

This modest shop has been a showcase for cool Belgian fashion. Martine Goethals has stocked radical clothes by Antwerp Six designers since the late 1980s and continues to look out for young talent emerging from Belgian fashion schools. Local women come here for silk dresses, understated jackets and thick winter sweaters.

184 GARE DE ROBE

Leopold II Laan 47-A
North Bruges ③
+32 (0)50 33 39 99
garederobe.be

A friendly fashion store located in an industrial building on the edge of town. It stocks stylish, wearable clothes by French and Belgian designers, such as Nathalie Vleeschouwer, FAM and knitwear brand La Femme Garniture. The store also has a small selection of shoes, handmade jewellery and perfume.

185 FRESH

Sint-Jakobsstraat 30
Historic Centre ①
+32 (0)472 81 54 49
freshbrugge.com

A cool lifestyle store for men and women in the heart of Bruges with an inspiring range of streetwear, bags, sneakers and accessories. The friendly owner sells some unique lines like quirky Polish sock brand Many Mornings. He also displays graphic art by young locals.

The 5 most creative
CONCEPT STORES

186 **GOÛTS ET COULEURS**
Ezelstraat 1 and 5
Historic Centre ①
+32 (0)50 69 82 83
gouts-et-couleurs.be

Interior designers Ester De Vestele and Bob Waterschoot have two small shops in Bruges dedicated mainly to Nordic design. One shop focuses on the latest trends in chairs, tables, lamps and vases by brands such as Hay, Ferm Living and Muuto. The other shop two doors down sells affordable accessories including candles, jewellery and cards.

187 **MAIS OUI**
Academiestraat 12
Historic Centre ①
+32 (0)50 69 81 40
mais-oui.be

Sisters Charlotte and Emmanuelle travel widely to find young, contemporary brands they admire by French, Danish and American designers. They display them in a little shop alongside their personal pick of ceramics, cushions and jewellery.

186 GOÛTS ET COULEURS

188 JŪTTU

Noordzandstraat 54
Historic Centre ②
+32 (0)50 33 10 06
juttu.be

The name looks Finnish, but Jūttu is a pure Belgian concept. The store opened in 2015 in a row of three gabled houses with a spacious interior decorated in hip Nordic style. Jūttu sells an inspiring mix of clothes, watches, plants and books. The focus is on small emerging brands with a unique identity like Anerkjendt from Denmark, Cluse from The Netherlands and Antwrp from Belgium.

189 ONLIFE CULTURE

Noordzandstraat 85
Historic Centre ②
+32 (0)472 81 63 90

Two locals opened this innovative concept store in 2017. The aim is to bring together ten young start-ups in a space where they can test out their concepts. The start-ups include an emerging fashion brand, a local artist, a recording studio and a food bar, as well as a hairdresser.

190 DUKA MOODSTORE

Wijngaardstraat 14
Begijnhof Quarter ⑤
+32 (0)478 98 79 10
duka-store.be

This little store occupies a whitewashed house near the Begijnhof. The owner sells handmade woollen scarves and hats by Belgian and French designers, along with eco-friendly T-shirts, jewellery and a small selection of art books. You can also perch on a corner bench upstairs with a coffee and a slice of tart.

The 5 best

VINTAGE SHOPS

191 **BROCANTE CAFÉ**
Langestraat 57
Sint-Anna Quarter ④
+32 (0)494 85 73 95
brocantecafe.com

Robbe and Joke have created a relaxed antique store where they sell old objects picked up in house sales. They claim everything in the shop is for sale expect the cash register. You might fall for a vintage stool, a plaster saint or a battered Belgian road sign. The owners also serve coffee and rare Belgian beers.

192 **VIE DE VUE**
Hoogstraat 40
Historic Centre ①
+32 (0)50 70 60 70
viedevue.be

A rambling antique store filled with nostalgic objects, like wooden skates, plaster saints, mounted animal heads and empty glass jars to plant a terrarium inside. It's a friendly place to browse with a neat price label attached to each item.

193 **SELECTED BY FRANÇOISE**
Ezelstraat 100
North Bruges ③
+32 (0)50 33 71 04
selectedbyfrancoise.be

Françoise Poulain runs a stylish vintage store in the trendy Ezelstraat. She's quite choosy in what she sells. You find almost new designer clothes and accessories by expensive brands like Dries Van Noten, Paul Smith and Sophie D'Hoore. But nothing trashy.

194 BROCANTE ROYAL

Leopold II-laan 43-45
North Bruges ③
+32 (0)50 33 78 38

A former garage on the edge of town is crammed with a vast collection of dusty antiques. You find stuffed foxes, Chinese vases, framed photographs and chandeliers hung from the roof. Maybe you will come across something exotic to take back home.

195 MADAM MIM

Hoogstraat 29
Historic Centre ①
+32 (0)50 61 55 05
madammim.be

Madam Mim opened her vintage store in 2011 in a striking step gable house painted red. She trawls flea markets, fairs and house sales to find old stuff to sell, like sunglasses, dresses, lace, family photographs and boxes of buttons.

192 VIE DE VUE

5 *interesting*
DESIGN STORES

196 **SERENDIPITY**
Sint-Jakobsstraat 56
Historic Centre ①
+32 (0)50 66 53 05
serendipity-store.be

Interior designer Anne Janssens opened her inspiring little concept store in 2017 in a gabled corner house opposite the Sint-Jakobskerk. She brings together a relaxed mix of rustic and contemporary objects including ceramics, cushions and perfume.

196 SERENDIPITY

197 CALLEBERT DESIGN

Wollestraat 25
Historic Centre ②
+32 (0)50 33 50 61
callebert.be

Not everything in Bruges is old. The design shop callebert is a favourite address for locals hunting for contemporary style. Founded back in 1948, the shop sells furniture by Italian designers, shiny kitchen equipment, quirky gadgets and wooden toys.

198 SKØNE

Zilverstraat 8
Historic Centre ②
+32 (0)487 20 52 55
skone.be

Interior architect Sven De Vuyst opened a beautiful shop in 2017 dedicated to contemporary Scandinavian design. He stocks the latest interior trends by brands like Muuto, &tradition and Handvärk.

199 LA STANZA DI STEFANIE

Ezelstraat 43
North Bruges ③
+32 (0)473 52 61 90
lastanzadistefanie.com

Stefanie sells a selection of Belgian and Italian design objects in a small shop opposite the Karmelietenkerk. Her selection includes wooden bowls, art books, perfumes and Belgian linen cushions.

200 MUNT

Muntplein 2
Historic Centre ②
+32 (0)50 33 25 71
munt.be

This stylish interior design store occupies an impressive mansion on the quiet Muntplein. Several rooms are decorated with furniture and objects by Belgian and Scandinavian brands. You can also drink coffee or a glass of wine on a quiet terrace at the back.

The 5 best

ANTIQUE DEALERS

201 **DEPOT D'O**
Riddersstraat 21
Historic Centre ①
+32 (0)495 23 65 95
depotdo.be

You stumble across the strangest objects in this mysterious antique shop. It might be a vintage radio, a cluster of wooden mushrooms or a plastic human body once used in anatomy classes.

202 **ATELIER PAPAGENO**
Vlamingstraat 52
Historic Centre ①
+32 (0)50 33 05 94
antiek-vanmullem.be

Bas Van Mullen skilfully restores antique furniture in a cluttered workshop near the city theatre. He also sells furniture and paintings in a small corner shop inherited from his parents. The shop name is inspired by the 1980 statue in front of the theatre representing Papageno from Mozart's Magic Flute.

203 **ROCOCO**
Wollestraat 9
Historic Centre ②
+32 (0)50 34 04 72
rococobrugge.be

Mieke Brack's lace shop has been selling authentic Bruges lace since 1834. It occupies a romantic 19th-century house decorated with shiny tiles and wrought iron details. The creepy animated model of a lace maker in the bay window makes it look like a tourist trap. But the lace on sale is handmade in Bruges using traditional methods.

204 CARLO BONTE

Kardinaal
Mercierstraat 20
North Bruges ③
+32 (0)50 33 23 55
carlobonte.be

Located in a warehouse just outside the Ezelpoort city gate, Carlo Bonte holds regular auctions of paintings and furniture. He specialises in Chinese art, including precious Ming vases brought back to Belgium by missionaries and railway engineers.

205 YANNICK DE HONDT

Sint-Salvators-
kerkhof 9
Historic Centre ②
+32 (0)475 65 30 58
yannickdehondt.be

Yannick De Hondt sells mysterious objects in a small brick house facing the Cathedral. He collects old European objects like painted pottery, Dutch Delftware and Gothic stone capitals rescued from demolished churches. But his real passion is rare African art.

201 DEPOT D'O

The 5 best shops for JEWELLERY *and* ACCESSORIES

206 GINKGO ICHO
Mariastraat 12
Historic Centre ②
+32 (0)50 74 33 48
ginkgojewels.com

Jonas Maes creates simple handmade jewellery in an old shop in the Mariastraat. His necklaces, rings and silver armbands are displayed in original settings. Some are laid out on ancient wooden beams. Others are placed on top of old LP records.

207 KINGIN
Ezelstraat 27
North Bruges ③
+32 (0)50 34 19 09
kingin.be

Nikolaas and Nathalie make elegant jewellery in a white step-gable house. The modest space is occupied by their workbench and a long wood counter where they lay out their creations.

208 GINKGO
Walplein 21
Begijnhof Quarter ⑤
+32 (0)479 26 94 89
ginkgojewels.com

This friendly jewellery shop near the Halve Maan brewery sells handmade silver rings, necklaces and bracelets. You can watch the makers at work at a wooden bench in the back of the shop. Some pieces are simple designs, while others are inspired by natural forms.

209 **HOET**

Vlamingstraat 19
Historic Centre ①
+32 (0)50 33 50 02
hoet.eu

When Patrick Hoet took over his mother's optician shop, he decided it was time to do something different. He now sells bright, distinctive eyewear in a stunning interior in the historic centre. Hoet often approaches Belgian artists and designers to create original styles for his brand Theo. Former customers include Bill Gates and Elton John.

210 **VALÉRIE V.**

Langerei 68
Sint-Gillis Quarter ③
+32 (0)50 34 38 03
valeriev.be

Valérie Van Maele studied jewellery at the acclaimed Academy of Fine Arts in Antwerp. She now makes unique necklaces and rings in a workshop located in a 16th-century canalside house. Phone ahead to book an appointment.

The 5 most

ORIGINAL SHOPS

211 FREDERIEK VAN PAMEL

Ezelstraat 33
North Bruges ③
+32 (0)50 34 44 80
frederiekvanpamel.be

Bruges florist Frederiek Van Pamel has built up a reputation for stunning floral arrangements. He moved in 2017 into an 18th-century town house where he has created a mysterious warren of rooms displaying exotic floral bouquets, stylish house plants, gardening tools and design books.

212 HUIS STANDAERT

Witte Leer-touwersstraat 48
Historic Centre ②
+32 (0)50 33 27 32
polstandaert.be

Pol Standaert runs an antique reproduction workshop founded by his grandfather in 1913. He creates ornamental fireplaces, plaster cast statues and architectural mouldings. You can admire a selection of his work in the family's handsome 16th-century Bruges mansion.

213 'T APOSTELIENTJE

Balstraat 11
Sint-Anna Quarter ④
+32 (0)50 33 78 60
apostelientje.be

Anne Thys sells authentic handmade Bruges lace in a romantic shop near the Jeruzalemkerk. She stocks the finest examples in a cluttered interior filled with oil paintings, framed samples and vintage lamps. Her customers include local aristocratic families looking for a lace tablecloth or a vintage shawl.

214 CHOCOLATE BROTHERS

Mariastraat 34
Historic Centre ②
chocolatebrothers.be

Three local chocolate makers came up with the idea of opening a chocolate workshop during a trip to Costa Rica in 2017. They took over a former lace shop with a beautiful tiled floor and installed some old machinery to demonstrate the art of chocolate production. Their aim is not just to sell their chocolate but to improve living conditions for farmers.

215 THE BOX BRUGGE

Academiestraat 14
Historic Centre ①
theboxvlaanderen.be/brugge

Several small rooms in the 15th-century Poortersloge have been turned into a store where local designers can launch their products. Featured start-ups include fashion designers, photographers and graphic artists. Worth a look if you are looking for an unusual gift.

211 FREDERIEK VAN PAMEL

5 shops for
HANDMADE CRAFTS

216 MAUD BEKAERT
Sint-Clarastraat 40
Sint-Gillis Quarter ③
+32 (0)475 26 95 58
maudbekaert.be

Maud Bekaert is a talented sculptor who specialises in letters carved in stone and rusted steel. She works in a little studio in a quiet back street where she chisels words into slabs of distinctive Belgian bluestone. She also creates stylish house numbers and even private gravestones. Her shop is only open on Fridays and Saturdays.

216 MAUD BEKAERT

217 ADOLPHE SAX & CIE

Gistelsesteenweg 97
Suburbs ⑦
+32 (0)497 55 55 85
adolphesax.be

Saxophone technician Karel was a funeral director before he opened his unique shop in 2012. Located in an elegant art nouveau house just outside the old town, it's a friendly, relaxed place filled with old and new saxophones. You can drop in to chat with the owner, try out an instrument and even borrow one for a few weeks.

218 SIMBOLIK

Katelijnestraat 139
South Bruges ⑤
+32 (0)495 30 70 56
simbolik.be

Nathalie Belprez is one of many skilled people in Bruges who like to work with their hands. She has a studio near a city gate where she creates handwritten calligraphy on paper, stone and linen sheets.

219 SHOERECRAFTING

Langestraat 13
Sint-Anna Quarter ④
+32 (0)50 33 81 01
shoerecrafting.be

Luc Decuyper opened his shoe repair shop in 1989 after learning the craft of leather working at the Delvaux factory in Brussels. He lovingly repairs old leather shoes in his workshop using traditional techniques.

220 ALFA PAPYRUS

Eekhoutstraat 25
Historic Centre ②
+32 (0)50 33 03 12
alfapapyrus.be

A little shop furnished with an old counter, wooden shelves and drawers to pull out. The owner stocks elegant notebooks, handmade sheets of paper, wrapping paper, rubber stamps and quirky postcards.

CONCERTGEBOUW

60 BUILDINGS TO ADMIRE

5 places to find

NEW ARCHITECTURE

221 CONCERTGEBOUW

't Zand 34
't Zand Quarter ⑥
+32 (0)50 47 69 99
concertgebouw.be

It's hard to find any modern architecture in Bruges, but not everything is Gothic or neo-Gothic. The most controversial new building is the rust red Concertgebouw built in 2002 by Ghent architects Paul Robbrecht and Hilde Daem. The Concertgebouw Circuit takes you backstage and into hidden corners to discover the architecture, acoustics and art.

222 COLLEGE OF EUROPE

Verversdijk 16
Historic Centre ①
+32 (0)50 47 71 11
coleurope.eu

Local heritage groups were horrified in 2007 when the College of Europe added a modern extension at the back of a 17th-century Jesuit school. Designed by Brussels architect Xaveer de Geyter, the simple white structure is based on a geometrical pattern of white cement panels.

223 SINT-ANDRIES LIBRARY

Gistelsesteenweg 524
Suburbs ⑦
+32 (0)50 72 70 50

Antwerp architects Studio Farris created an astonishing modern library in the Bruges suburbs in 2015. They did so by adding a modern extension with raw rust steel walls to the existing white 19th-century library building.

224 RIJKSARCHIEF

Predikherenrei 4-A
Historic Centre ②
+32 (0)50 33 72 88
arch.be

Opened in 2012, the new Rijksarchief (state archive) was designed by Bruges firm Salens Architecten. It occupies a smart red brick building with a wavy roof designed to look like a pile of crumpled pages. The main building is attached to an old convent now used for exhibitions.

225 GROENINGEMUSEUM

Dijver 12
Historic Centre ②
+32 (0)50 44 87 43
visitbruges.be

The Groeninge art museum was redesigned in 2003 by architects 51N4E. The Brussels-based firm transformed the 1930s museum by introducing bare white walls and deep red carpets the colour of a Virgin's gown. The result is visually striking and occasionally shocking. But then Flemish art was never meant to be comforting.

223 SINT-ANDRIES LIBRARY

The 5 most
SECRET CHAPELS

226 ONZE-LIEVE-VROUW-VAN-BLINDEKENS CHAPEL

Kreupelenstraat 8
't Zand Quarter ⑥
visitbruges.be

The little chapel of Our Lady of the Blind was built in the 17th century on the site of a much older chapel. It contains a 15th-century carved Madonna, a 17th-century altar painting of the blind praying to the Virgin, and, hanging above the chapel, a model of a ship.

227 GRUUTHUSE CHAPEL

AT: GRUUTHUSEMUSEUM, ROOM 16
Dijver 17
Historic Centre ②
visitbruges.be

A covered passage in the Gruuthuse-museum leads to a small private chapel overlooking Onze-Lieve-Vrouwekerk. It was built for Lodewijk van Gruuthuse in 1472 so he could attend Mass without leaving his palace. The chapel is a secret, magical spot with tiny skylight windows and a vaulted wooden roof decorated with gilded paper flowers. Closed for renovation until spring 2019.

228 KARTUIZERINNEN-KERK

Kartuizerinnen-straat 4
Historic Centre ②

A quiet lane almost no one goes down leads to a chapel built in 1632 by Carthusian monks. It was converted into a war memorial in 1927, with plaques added later on the outside wall listing the dead of two world wars.

229 GREEK ORTHODOX CHAPEL

Ezelstraat 85
North Bruges ③
+32 (0)476 49 95 77
brugge.orthodoxia.be

A small door on Ezelstraat leads into a chapel no one knows. Built in the 15th century, the Sint-Joos chapel was given to the Greek Orthodox Church in 2007. A door at the far end of the entrance hall leads into a hidden garden surrounded by almshouses.

230 ENGLISH CONVENT CHAPEL

Carmersstraat 83-85
Sint-Anna Quarter ④
+32 (0)50 33 24 24
the-english-convent.be

Established in 1629 by Catholic nuns fleeing from England, the English Convent is one of the strangest spots in Bruges. Ring the bell in the courtyard and wait for one of the elderly nuns to appear. She leads you down a bare corridor and into a baroque chapel with an impressive dome and an altar made from 23 types of rare marble.

226 ONZE-LIEVE-VROUW-VAN-BLINDEKENS CHAPEL

5 *impressive*
TRADING HOUSES

231 **OOSTERLINGENHUIS**
Oosterlingenplein 4
Historic Centre ①

The former trading house of the Hanseatic League stands on a quiet square away from the crowds. Built in 1478, the building was originally used to store fur and grain from the Baltic, beer from Bremen, and wines from the Rhineland. Patched up over the years, the building is now occupied by a hotel.

232 **HUIS TER BEURZE**
Vlamingstraat 35
Historic Centre ①
huisterbeurze.be

The tall stone building known as Ter Beurze stands on the site of a 13th-century inn run by the Van der Beurse family. The inn became the financial centre of mediaeval Bruges (leading to the word *beurs* for a stock exchange). Taken over in 1397 by Venetian merchants, it is now occupied by a local radio station.

233 HUIS DE LA TORRE

Spanjaardstraat 16
Historic Centre ①

A tall stone house with a fortified façade was built around 1500 for merchants from Castile. It stands near the shady Spaanse Loskaai, or Spanish Quay, where ships unloaded Spanish wool, hides and oranges.

234 GENUESE LOGE

Vlamingstraat 33
Historic Centre ①

Built in 1399, the Genoa trading house has miraculously survived intact. It originally served merchants who shipped fruit, spices and alum. But the Genoans eventually moved to Antwerp and the building was used for other purposes. It was a cloth hall, hotel, reading room and cinema, but is now home to the Frietmuseum (chip museum) of all things.

235 HOF BLADELIN

Naaldenstraat 19
Historic Centre ①
+32 (0)472 01 74 51
visitbruges.be

Peter Bladelin's beautiful 15th-century mansion is normally hidden behind a high brick wall, but you can see the secret renaissance hedge garden through the iron grille to the left of the entrance. The house was acquired by the Medici banking family in the late 15th century.

The 5 most

HIDDEN ALMSHOUSES

236 GODSHUIS SINT-JOZEF

Nieuwe Gentweg 24-32
Begijnhof Quarter ⑤

One of 46 almshouses dotted around Bruges, the Godshuis Sint-Jozef was built in the 17th century as a home for the poor, alongside a second almshouse called De Meulenaere. Hidden from the street by high whitewashed walls, the gardens are planted with ancient trees, rose beds and low box hedges.

237 ROOMS CONVENT

Katelijnestraat 9-19
Begijnhof Quarter ⑤

Most people walk straight past the small arched door on the busy Katelijnestraat. It leads down a narrow covered lane to the oldest surviving almshouse in Bruges. Founded in 1330, the Rooms Convent originally accommodated seven poor women in tiny whitewashed houses overlooking a walled garden.

238 GODSHUIS DE FONTAINE

Zwarte Leertouwersstraat 82
Astridpark Quarter ②

A small entrance leads into a quiet garden surrounded by whitewashed houses and a small chapel. Count Paul-Bernard de la Fontaine founded this almshouse in 1636 to accommodate 12 wounded or retired soldiers.

239 GODSHUIS DE MOOR

Boeveriestraat 52-62
South Bruges ⑤

This row of 13 neat white houses was founded in 1480 by the city official Donaas de Moor and his wife Adriana de Vos. The houses were given to members of the guilds of carpenters, masons and coopers, each of them given three, while the remaining four went to a hospice dedicated to Saint Julian.

240 GODSHUIS MARIUS VOET

Kammakers-straat 13-17
't Zand Quarter ⑥

A row of three almshouses was gifted by Marius Voet in 1672 to accommodate three blind women. The building is decorated with the Voet family coat of arms, which includes three little feet, a play on the word *voet* (foot). An arched gate leads into a narrow lane next to secret gardens planted with tulips and roses.

236 GODSHUIS SINT-JOZEF

5 FORGOTTEN CHURCHES
worth a visit

241 **JERUZALEMKERK**
Peperstraat 3
Sint-Anna Quarter ④
+32 (0)50 33 88 83
www.adornes.org

This mysterious private church was built by the Adornes family in 1429. It lies in a quiet neighbourhood, away from the crowds, so you might be the only visitor. Modelled on the Church of the Holy Sepulchre in Jerusalem, the interior is on two levels, with family relics, a strange Crucifixion and a replica of Christ's tomb in a dark crypt you have to crawl inside.

242 **SINT-BASILIUSKAPEL**
Burg
Historic Centre ②

A small door in the corner of Burg square leads into an ancient chapel dedicated to Saint Basil. Most tourists miss this chapel as they head to the gaudy upper chapel with the relic of the Holy Blood. Built of rough stone in romanesque style, the lower chapel is a dark, mysterious place with carved heads buried in the walls.

243 **SINT-WALBURGA-KERK**
Sint-Maartensplein
Historic Centre ①

Begun in 1619, this huge baroque church is one of three in Flanders built by the Jesuit architect Peter Huyssens in the style of the Gesù church in Rome. The pulpit, designed by Artus Quellin of Antwerp in 1667, is particularly impressive.

244 MAGDALENAKERK

Schaarstraat
Astridpark Quarter ②

Thomas Harper King, a British architect who settled in Bruges, designed this church in 1853 following neo-Gothic principles laid down by the British architect A.W. Pugin. Now rather dilapidated, the church is sometimes used for art exhibitions.

245 SINT-ANNAKERK

Sint-Annaplein
Sint-Anna Quarter ④

Located on a quiet square, Sint-Annakerk is a simple church with a thin spire. The dark interior is furnished with baroque wood panelling and a handsome marble rood screen. Other churches in Bruges often have a neglected air, but someone here polishes the brass fittings with fanatical energy.

241 JERUZALEMKERK

The 5

OLDEST HOUSES

246 **GENTHOF 7**

Genthof 7
Historic Centre ①

Built in about 1500, this is one of just two authentic wood-fronted houses in Bruges. The others are all fake, but this house is faced with blackened wooden boards that have survived more than 500 years.

247 **WOODEN HOUSE IN KORTEWINKEL**

NEXT TO:
Kortewinkel 2
Historic Centre ①

This ancient building has an authentic 16th-century wooden façade. But no front door. The entrance is located at the back of the house, reached through a gate around the corner at Vlamingstraat 90.

248 **DE ZOMERE**

Oude Zomerstraat 2
Historic Centre ②

A lane lined with garages leads to a tall narrow house with a carved stone giving the construction date as 1479. Known as De Zomere, this is one of the few authentic houses to have survived from the late middle ages. It is now owned by a calligraphy collector who added the beautiful carved stone next to the entrance.

249 OUD WATERHUIS

NEAR:
Hendrik Consciencelaan 25
't Zand Quarter ⑥

Half hidden in the trees, the Oud Waterhuis is not easy to find. Yet this forgotten relic was ranked in the 16th century as one of the seven wonders of Bruges. Dating from 1394, it raised water from the moat to supply all the city's water pumps and fountains.

250 HUIS JACOB CNOOP

Vlamingstraat 51
Historic Centre ①

This strange late-Gothic house was built for the goldsmith Jacob Cnoop, whose daughter married the painter Gerard David. Built in 1516, Cnoop's house has perhaps the most eccentric gable in Bruges.

248 **DE ZOMERE**

The 5 most

ROMANTIC BRIDGES

251 **LEEUWBRUG**
Leeuwstraat
Historic Centre ①

Located in a lost, forgotten corner of the city, this old stone bridge is one of the most beautiful in Bruges. It is decorated with two large lions holding shields carved with the letter B for Bruges. They date from 1629, but the Lion Bridge is much older.

251 **LEEUWBRUG**

252 MEEBRUG

Steenhouwersdijk
Historic Centre ②

This ancient stone bridge was built in 1390 by Jan van Oudenaerde. The view from this bridge is one of the most romantic in Bruges, especially after dark when the streets around here are often deserted.

253 SLEUTELBRUG

Beenhouwersstraat
't Zand Quarter ⑥

Only a few people walk down the quiet canal leading to the Sleutelbrug. Built next to the little Minstrels' Chapel (Speelmanskapel), the ancient stone bridge dates back to 1331. It takes its name from a vanished brewery called De Sleutel, or The Key.

254 AUGUSTIJNENBRUG

Augustijnenrei
Historic Centre ①

The oldest bridge in Bruges, the Augustijnenbrug is a handsome three-arched stone bridge built in 1391 to provide Augustinian friars with a convenient crossing into the city. It is one of several historic bridges in Bruges with stone benches where merchants would display their goods on fine days.

255 DUINENBRUG

Langerei
Sint-Gillis Quarter ③

Located on a quiet stretch of the Langerei canal, the Duinenbrug is an unusual wooden drawbridge that can be raised to allow boats to pass. It takes its name from the nearby Duinenabdij (Abbey of the Dunes).

5 *impressive relics of the* CITY WALLS

256 FIRST CITY WALL
Augustijnenrei
Historic Centre ①

A short stretch of the original city wall built in 1127 has survived along the Augustijnenrei. It includes the remains of a brick tower in the back garden of a house that has its front door at Pieter Pourbusstraat 3.

257 EZELPOORT
Ezelstraat 122
North Bruges ③
visitbruges.be

Nothing remains of the 13th-century city defences apart from four stone gates and the moat. The rest was torn down in the 19th century to create a ring of landscaped parks. Built in 1297 and rebuilt in 1369, the rugged Ezelpoort (Donkey Gate) has two massive round turrets rising out of the moat.

258 KRUISPOORT
Langestraat 191
East Bruges ④
visitbruges.be

The Kruispoort has immensely thick stone walls built by Jan van Oudenaerde and Maarten van Leuven in 1401. A stone plaque next to the gate is carved in a Gothic script that looks ancient. But it is a relatively modern addition. It records that German troops fled through this gate on 19 October 1918.

259 GENTPOORT

Gentpoortvest
South Bruges ⑤
+32 (0)50 44 87 43
visitbruges.be

The Gentpoort, like the Kruispoort, was built in 1401 by Jan van Oudenaerde and Maarten van Leuven. It originally guarded the busy route from Ghent to Bruges. Now it is a quiet spot on the landscaped ramparts.

260 SMEDENPOORT

Smedenstraat
't Zand Quarter ⑥
visitbruges.be

The massive Smedenpoort has been guarding one of the city's main entrances since 1368. It was destroyed by the German army in 1944, but faithfully rebuilt and recently repainted yellow, as it would have been in the Middle Ages. The gate has always been a traffic bottleneck, but the city recently came up with a smart solution by adding two footbridges.

260 SMEDENPOORT

The 5 strangest relics of
VANISHED BUILDINGS

261 **SINT-DONAAS-KATHEDRAAL**
BELOW:
CROWNE PLAZA HOTEL
Burg 10
Historic Centre ②
+32 (0)50 44 68 44

A dusty patch of ground on the north side of Burg square was once the site of the great cathedral of Sint-Donaas. It was demolished in 1799 by French Republicans, leaving a sad empty space in the heart of Bruges. All that remains are 11th-century foundations hidden in the basement of the Crowne Plaza Hotel. Ask at the reception desk and they will show you where to go.

262 **PRINSENHOF**
AT: HOTEL DUKES' PALACE
Prinsenhof 8
Historic Centre ②
+32 (0)50 44 78 88
hoteldukespalace.com

The Prinsenhof was the scene of two extraordinary Burgundian banquets in the 15th century. The first in 1430 marked the wedding of Philip the Good and Isabella of Portugal, the second 38 years later celebrated the wedding of Charles the Bold to Margaret of York. The palace was rebuilt in the 19th century in French neo-Gothic style, leaving almost nothing of the original.

263 ZUIDPOORT

Blinde Ezelstraat 1
Historic Centre ②

Most people who walk down Blinde Ezelstraat miss the plaque on the wall with the inscription *Dit was 't Zuidpoort* (This was the South Gate). It marks one of the gates into a castle that stood on Burg. But all that's left is an iron bolthole embedded in the wall.

264 WATERHALLE

Arentshof
Historic Centre ②

The great 13th-century Waterhalle has vanished without a trace. Constructed over a canal to allow flat-bottomed boats to unload, it was demolished in 1786, leaving just two unexplained stone columns in the little park Arentshof.

265 CROSSBOWMEN TOWER

Sint-Jorisstraat 71
Sint-Gillis Quarter ③

All the remains of the Crossbowmen's guildhall is a solitary stone tower dating from 1508. It now forms part of a flamboyant neo-Gothic building decorated with turrets, gables and miniature castles.

263 ZUIDPOORT

The 5 most surprising
FAKE BUILDINGS

266 **BONIFACIUSBRUG**
Arentshof
Historic Centre ②

Everyone knows the little hump-backed bridge called the Bonifaciusbrug. It is one of the most photographed spots in Bruges, with the canal gently lapping at the crumbling brick foundations. It looks ancient, but it was actually built in 1910 in a fake mediaeval style that incorporated some old gravestones.

266 BONIFACIUSBRUG

267 PROVINCIAAL HOF

Markt 3
Historic Centre ②

Built on the site of the ancient Waterhalle, the Provinciaal Hof looks mediaeval, but it was built between 1887 and 1921. The flamboyant white stone building was designed by local architect Louis Delacenserie, who borrowed ideas from the 15th-century Gruuthuse and from the town hall on Burg.

268 VLAMINGSTRAAT 38

Vlamingstraat 38
Historic Centre ①

The house with the black wooden front at Vlamingstraat 38 looks as if it dates from the Middle Ages. But it is a copy of a building in Pieter Pourbus' *Portrait of Jacquemyne Buuck* in the Groeningemuseum. The house was built by a local architect as recently as 1963.

269 RIJKSNORMAAL-SCHOOL

Sint-Jorisstraat 69-71
Sint-Gillis Quarter ③

One of the oddest buildings in Bruges, the Rijksnormaalschool stands on the site of the crossbowmen's guildhall. Designed by Louis Delacenserie in the 1880s, it combines neo-Gothic brickwork with flamboyant wrought iron details. Originally a school, the gloomy, dilapidated building is now a university campus.

270 HISTORIUM

Markt 1
Historic Centre ②
+32 (0)50 27 03 11
historium.be

The Historium occupies a grey stone building on Markt that looks as if it has been around for centuries. But it is no more authentic than the virtual reality experience inside. It was built in the 1920s in the elaborate Burgundian Gothic style of 15th-century Bruges.

5
ECCENTRIC BUILDINGS

271 LUCAS-HUYS

Minderbroedersstraat 10
Astridpark Quarter ②

The mysterious Lucas House is made from fragments of other buildings, including a wooden façade believed to come from a house in Brussels. A puzzling verse in Dutch picked out in gilt letters begins, "Here I built/this Flemish dwelling place/to some a delight/to some a disgrace."

272 ZWART HUIS

Kuipersstraat 23
Historic Centre ①
+32 (0)50 69 11 40
bistrozwarthuis.be

You can still read the faded word CINEMA on an ancient Gothic building known as the Zwart Huis (Black House). Built as a merchant's house in 1482, this impressive building was converted into a cinema in 1919. But the last film was screened here in 2017.

273 THE GOLDSMITH'S HOUSE

Vlamingstraat 100
Historic Centre ①

An elaborate oriel window projects out from a house next to the Vlamingbrug. This beautiful example of Flemish late-Gothic brickwork was commissioned in 1514 by the goldsmith Herman van Oudvelde, who probably worked at the window looking out on the canal.

274 GOTHIC CHIMNEY

Noordstraat
Begijnhof Quarter ⑤

A tall Gothic chimney is all that survives of the ancient Bogarden convent. Propped up with a buttress, it is now incorporated into the neo-Gothic wing of the 19th-century city art academy. The tiny interior is occasionally used for exhibitions of student art projects.

275 THE HOUSE WITH THE DRAGONS' HEADS

Sint-Amandsstraat 7
Historic Centre ②

One of the strangest houses in Bruges stands in the Sint-Amandsstraat. It is a dark brick building with a fortified look. Dating back to the 13th century, it was rebuilt in 1573 and again in the 19th century, when the arrow slits were added along with curious spy mirrors and iron railings decorated with dragons' heads.

273 THE GOLDSMITH'S HOUSE

The 5
STRANGEST BRIDGES

276 **KANAALEILAND BRIDGE**
Bargeweg
South Bruges ⑤

The Kanaaleiland used to be a desolate spot where coach tourists were dropped off. But in 2002 the city decided to create an impressive entry point here, like a mediaeval city gate. The Rotterdam architects West 8 came up with a bold plan for an undulating red metal bridge across the old moat.

277 **CONZETT BRIDGE**
Boninvest
South Bruges ⑦

In 2002, when Bruges was cultural capital of Europe, the city constructed several modern buildings, including the striking new footbridge at the far end of Coupure. Designed by the Swiss engineer Jürg Conzett, it can be raised to allow boats to pass.

278 HOSPITAL BRIDGE

Zonnekemeers
Begijnhof Quarter ⑤

A curious covered wooden bridge crosses a quiet cobbled street near the Sint-Janshospitaal. It looks like a mediaeval gate decorated with two turrets, but in fact dates from 1938 when it was built to take hospital patients to a clinic on the other side of the street. The ramps leading to the bridge were demolished in the 1990s, leaving just this bridge no one can cross.

279 GRUUTHUSE CHAPEL BRIDGE

AT: GRUUTHUSEMUSEUM, ROOM 13
Dijver 17
Historic Centre ②
visitbruges.be

A little bridge crosses the narrow lane between the Gruuthuse mansion and Onze-Lieve-Vrouwekerk. It was built in 1472 to allow the Gruuthuse family to reach their private chapel in the church without having to go out into the street. Closed for renovation until spring 2019.

280 SCHEEPSDALE BRIDGE

Scheepsdalelaan
Suburbs ⑦

A stunning modern tilt bridge opened in 2011 on the shipping canal north of Bruges. It replaced a historic rotating iron bridge that was demolished despite protests. The new bridge is particularly impressive at night when it is lit up.

GROENEREI

60 PLACES TO DISCOVER BRUGES

The 5 most

HIDDEN PARKS

281 **PARK SEBRECHTS**
NEXT TO:
Oude Zak 55 and Beenhouwersstraat 24
Historic Centre ①

Not many people know about this forgotten park hidden behind an abandoned doctor's mansion. Acquired by the city in 1980, the park has ancient trees, a children's playground and an iron gate leading to a quiet canal. As you wander through the grounds, you get unexpected views of the city's Gothic churches and ancient towers.

282 **PASTOOR VAN HAECKEPLANTSOEN**
NEXT TO:
Ezelstraat 123
North Bruges ③

This park is a real hidden secret, even to locals. It once belonged to a large town house owned by a local judge, but the house was torn down in the 1960s to build an apartment block, leaving just the overgrown garden and a small, dark pond. The park is named after an eccentric local priest who carried out exorcisms and attended black masses.

283 **KONINGIN ASTRIDPARK**

Park
Astridpark Quarter ②

The Koningin Astridpark was planted in 1852 in English landscape style on the site of a demolished monastery. With its blue and yellow bandstand, winding paths and ponds, it is one of the most romantic parks in Bruges.

284 **GENTPOORTVEST**

Gentpoortvest
South Bruges ⑤

Most tourists never discover the romantic landscaped park on the edge of the city moat. The oldest green space was created on the site of the ramparts in 1853. The work was done by the Belgian landscape gardener Egidius Rosseels, who had already impressed the city with his design for the Koningin Astridpark.

285 **SINCFAL**

Calvariebergstraat
Sint-Gillis Quarter ③

This quiet park on the edge of the old town is landscaped in romantic style with old trees, winding paths and a stream. The park is surrounded by attractive brick houses built by a local housing association in the 1970s.

5
UNEXPECTED VIEWS

286 **GODSHUIS SPANOGHE GARDEN**
Katelijnestraat 8
Begijnhof Quarter ⑤

A little lane off the busy Katelijnestraat leads to a spot almost no one knows about. Go through the gate and you find whitewashed almshouses founded in 1680 by Francisca Spanoghe. They overlook a small park on the edge of the canal where you get an unexpected view of the ancient brick walls of the Sint-Janshospitaal rising out of the water.

287 **GRUUTHUSE WINDOW**
AT: GRUUTHUSEMUSEUM
Dijver 17
Historic Centre ②
visitbruges.be

You need to look closely to see a tiny Gothic window on the corner of the Gruuthuse palace. It was originally built to spot boats arriving at the landing stage below. Most people walk straight past the window when they visit the museum. Yet the view through the tiny opening is like a miniature Flemish painting.

288 SINT-JANSHUYS-MOLEN

Kruisvest 3
Sint-Anna Quarter ④

Tourists normally don't stray far from the centre, but it's worth taking a short 10-minute stroll out to the east side of Bruges. Here you can climb up to an ancient windmill on the ramparts for a fantastic view of the old roofs and spires of Bruges. The view takes in Onze-Lieve-Vrouwekerk, Sint-Salvatorkathedraal and the Belfry, as well as an ancient archery range.

289 PASSAGE BOURGOENSCH CRUYCE

NEXT TO:
Wollestraat 35
Historic Centre ②

A little lane on the busy Wollestraat leads to a small courtyard with a beautiful view across the canal to the historic buildings on Burg. A famous restaurant called Duc de Bourgogne occupies the white building opposite the courtyard.

290 HISTORIUM TOWER

Markt 1
Historic Centre ②
+32 (0)50 27 03 11
historium.be

A cramped staircase with 145 stone steps leads to a lookout point at the top of a tower high above Markt. Built in 1921 in the style of the 15th-century Poortersloge, the tower offers an impressive view of the old town. But it's quite a squeeze up the narrow stairs.

5 *charming*
SECRET GARDENS

291 **GROENINGEMUSEUM GARDEN**
Dijver 12
Historic Centre ②
+32 (0)50 44 87 43
visitbruges.be

The Groeningemuseum garden is a strangely quiet spot in the heart of the old city. It stands on the site of a mediaeval abbey demolished in 1803, leaving just a gate on Eeckhoutstraat and a mysterious Gothic arch in the garden.

292 **RODE NONNEN GARDEN**
Katelijnestraat 115
South Bruges ⑤

No one knows about this garden. Renovated and opened to the public in 2018, it lies hidden behind a high brick wall. Once tended by sisters of the Holy Redeemer Convent (known locally as the Red Nuns), it has been turned into a small public park with old trees, a garden chapel and a ruined gazebo. Open from dawn to dusk.

293 **GRAUWWERKERS-STRAAT GARDENS**
FACING:
Grauwwerkers-straat 31
Historic Centre ②

Most private gardens in Bruges are hidden, but you can admire a row of ten waterside gardens along the Grauwwerkersstraat. They belong to houses on Pottenmakersstraat with back gardens that run down to the canal. The owners have planted their modest plots in different formal styles.

294 HOF DE JONGHE

Langerei 75
Sint-Gillis Quarter ③

A narrow lane leads to a quiet, forgotten park called Hof de Jonghe. Planted with apple trees, it is home to three grazing sheep.

295 THE RUINED HOUSE

Pottenmakers-straat 18
Historic Centre ①

A ruined house in a quiet lane has been taken over by a local guerrilla gardener who lives a few doors away. It had been used as a place to dump rubbish until she turned it into a poetic spot with writing on the wall and a neat herb garden planted in the former front room.

295 THE RUINED HOUSE

The 5

NARROWEST LANES

296 **DE VETTE VISPOORT ALLEY**
Moerstraat 10
Historic Centre ①

A narrow passage off Moerstraat leads to a hidden 15th-century almshouse called De Vette Vispoort. Walk down to the end of the lane for an unexpected view of a canal.

297 **KIPSTRAAT**
Historic Centre ①

One of the narrowest lanes in Bruges meanders between high brick walls and an abandoned 19th-century Jesuit church. No one can explain why it is called Kipstraat, or Chicken Street.

298 **STROSTRAAT**
Sint-Anna Quarter ④

This mysterious cobbled lane runs between mellow brick walls near the Sint-Annakerk. The walls are too high to see what lies beyond, but you can sometimes glimpse a secret baroque garden through an open gate. Look out for the old gravestones used as paving at the end of the street.

299 HEMELRIJK

Sint-Anna Quarter ④

It feels as if you have left the city behind when you turn down the narrow lane Hemelrijk. The last surviving gravel road in Bruges, it takes you past high brick walls and old iron lampposts, almost like a country lane.

300 STOOFSTRAAT

South Bruges ⑤

Every tourist who comes to Bruges struggles down the crowded Katelijne-straat, but not many turn into the narrow alley called Stoofstraat. It is named after the medieval *stoven*, or bathhouses, once located here. An information panel on the wall gives a bit of history of these places which were possibly more like brothels than bathhouses.

5 *of the most*
QUIET CANALS

301 AUGUSTIJNENREI
Historic Centre ①

One of the most attractive quays in Bruges, Augustijnenrei once formed the northern edge of the city. It takes its name from an Augustinian friary with a chapel used by wealthy Spanish and Italian merchants. The friary was torn down after the French Revolution, leaving just a little square with lime trees where the chapel once stood.

302 **GOUDEN-HANDREI**

302 GOUDEN-HANDREI
Sint-Gillis Quarter ①③

Bruges still has a network of canals dating from the time when it was an important seaport. One of the most romantic is the Gouden-Handrei, a forgotten stretch of water with houses on the far side rising out of the water.

303 COUPURE
East Bruges ②④

The broad straight canal called Coupure was cut in 1753. Lined with modest houses, yachts and barges, it feels different from the older areas of the city. Locals sometimes say it looks like somewhere in the South of France, but that's maybe going too far.

304 SPEELMANSREI
't Zand Quarter ⑥

Not many people find this overgrown stretch of canal on the west side of town. It gets its name from a little 15th-century brick chapel once used by the Minstrels' Guild.

305 GROENEREI
Historic Centre ②

A ten-minute walk from the centre, this quiet canal is one of the most romantic in Bruges. It is best seen from the Peerdebrug, the Horse Bridge, looking back towards the Belfry. The waterway is even more romantic after dark, when old trees and creepers are lit up.

5 FORGOTTEN NEIGHBOURHOODS
to check out

306 **VERLOREN HOEK**
BEGIN AT:
Sint-Annakerk
Sint-Anna Quarter ④

The Verloren Hoek, or Lost Corner, lies on the edge of town, far from the crowds. It's a quiet, undiscovered quarter with modest workers' houses, whitewashed almshouses and hidden religious institutions. The main landmarks are three wooden windmills built on the ramparts to catch the wind.

307 **SINT-GILLIS QUARTER**
BEGIN AT:
Sint-Gilliskerk
Sint-Gillis Quarter ③

You soon escape the crowds in the quiet streets around the Sint-Gilliskerk. Most of the buildings in this quarter are workers' houses from the 16th century. The artist Hans Memling bought a house in 1480 in the Sint-Jorisstraat and was buried in 1494 next to the Sint-Gilliskerk.

308 SINT-ANNA QUARTER

BEGIN AT:
Sint-Annakerk
Sint-Anna Quarter ④

The quiet streets around the Sint-Annakerk have kept an authentic Bruges character. Here is where you discover the real Bruges where local people have lived for generations. The church is surrounded by quiet cobbled lanes lined with workers' homes and almshouses. The odd tower of the Jeruzalemkapel adds a mysterious touch to the neighbourhood.

309 BEURSPLEIN QUARTER

BEGIN AT:
Smedenpoort
't Zand Quarter ⑥

A quiet, forgotten corner of Bruges lies to the west of 't Zand. It has no tourist sites, so almost no one goes there. Yet this modest neighbourhood has a particular charm, with old almshouses, small chapels and a romantic park planted along the ramparts.

310 KANAAL GENT-BRUGGE

BEGIN AT:
Bargeweg
South Bruges ⑤

Not many people know the old industrial quarter along the Bruges to Ghent canal. But this is an interesting area to explore on foot or by bike, with quiet towpaths, iron bridges and enormous barges heading to Zeebrugge. The most impressive buildings are the massive La Brugeoise power station from 1912, now an event venue, and the Bombardier train construction site.

The 5 most

UNEXPECTED STATUES

311 **HOMELESS JESUS**
Stalijzerstraat 19
Astridpark Quarter ②

A strange sculpture representing a homeless Jesus sleeping on a park bench was placed outside the Magdalenakerk in 2017. It is a copy of a work in Toronto by Canadian sculptor Timothy Schmalz. The Bruges police were alerted soon after the work was unveiled by a local who thought it was a real person.

312 **MICHELANGELO'S VIRGIN AND CHILD**
AT: ONZE-LIEVE-VROUWEKERK
Mariastraat
Historic Centre ②
+32 (0)50 44 87 11
visitbruges.be

A tiny sculpture by Michelangelo was brought back to Bruges in 1506 by the merchant Jan Mouscron, who acquired it from a bankrupt Italian. Carved soon after the famous *Pietà* in Rome, the work illustrates Michelangelo's soft and serene early style.

313 **DE GELIEFDEN**
Burg
Historic Centre ②

The artist couple Stefaan Depuydt and Livia Canestraro created a bronze statue of two lovers in the centre in Bruges in 2002. Located near the Stadhuis (city hall), where local couples get married, the statue has the word love in many languages etched into the base.

314 MARIEKE

Coupure
East Bruges ④

Shaded by trees, a bronze statue represents the girl in Jacques Brel's beautiful 1961 song *Marieke*. She was said to live 'between the towers of Bruges and Ghent'. In 1988, a local journalist persuaded the city to put up this statue of Marieke wearing a summer dress with bells hanging from her ears. Locals sometimes like to dress her in warmer clothes when winter comes around.

315 ONZE-LIEVE-VROUW MET DE INKTPOT

Burg
Historic Centre ②

A curious statue on the corner of the Stadhuis represents *Onze-Lieve-Vrouw met de Inktpot* (Our Lady of the Inkwell). She was the patron saint of clerks, and so protected the bureaucrats who worked in the town hall. The statue was carved in the 1960s to replace a lost original.

311 HOMELESS JESUS

5 beautiful
CARVED LETTERS

316 **SUNDIAL**
Jeruzalemstraat 57
Sint-Anna Quarter ④
pieterboudens.be

Stonemason Pieter Boudens revived the ancient craft of letter carving in stone more than 40 years ago. He created a beautiful sundial in 2002 to decorate the outside wall of a local social security office. The inscription reads *Alleen de schaduw sluipt verder* (Only the shadow creeps ahead).

317 **CALLIGRAPHY GATES**
Begijnenvest
Begijnhof Quarter ⑤

The American calligrapher Brody Neuenschwander, who lives in Bruges, designed the lettering of a poem cut into two wrought iron gates near the Begijnhof. Created in 2004, the gates are incorporated into a 19th-century brick wall built by the architect Louis Delacenserie. The holes in the iron plates allow you to see inside a private garden belonging to a care home.

317 **CALLIGRAPHY GATES**

318 THE GLASS SPHERE

Ezelstraat 81
North Bruges ③

A modest brick house in Ezelstraat is decorated with a strange inscription dating from its renovation by the city housing department in 2004. *De wereld is een bol van glas* (The world is a glass sphere), it reads in beautiful calligraphy, with the word *bol* replaced by a tiny glass ball.

319 NOTHING NEW

Greinschuurstraat 15
't Zand Quarter ⑥

Er is niets nieuws zonder de zon (There is nothing new without the sun), reads a carved stone on the wall of a house in West Bruges. The line comes from the poem *Winter* by the Flemish poet Herman De Coninck. The work was unveiled by the president of the local housing association in 2006.

320 I BLOW OUT THE MOON

Wervershof 11
Begijnhof Quarter ⑤

A lane near the Begijnhof leads to a complex of whitewashed workers' houses called Wervershof, built on the site of a 19th-century fort. The buildings were restored in 1996 by the housing association Domus Flandria and a stone memorial carved with words from a poem – *Ik blaas de maan uit en alleen de klaprozen geven licht* (I blow out the moon and the poppies are the only source of light).

The 5 most

CURIOUS SHRINES

321 **ANNAATJE VAN 'T PITJE SHRINE**
Carmersstraat 84
Sint-Anna Quarter ④

Dating from 1760, this strange Catholic shrine was put up to commemorate a local miracle in which a girl was tossed into a well. But the water at the bottom of the well had turned to ice and she survived the ordeal. The shrine incorporates a wooden Crucifixion, a Virgin and Child in a glass-fronted case and an ornate wooden canopy that helps to protect it from the rain.

321 ANNAATJE VAN 'T PITJE SHRINE

322 O.L.V. VAN EEUWIG DURENDE BIJSTAND

Groeninge 65
Begijnhof Quarter ⑤

A shrine in the cobbled lane Groeninge is dedicated to Our Lady of Perpetual Help. "To everyone who passes here/on foot or on horse/say 'Greeting to You, Mary'," it says. But take care as you stand here as the narrow lane is a popular route for horse-drawn carriages.

323 AVE MARIA

Peerdenstraat
Historic Centre ①

A strongly Catholic city, Bruges is dotted with small statues of the Virgin and Child, including a beautiful example next to the stone bridge Peerdenbrug. Often accompanied by the words Ave Maria, these little statues date from a time when the cult of the Virgin Mary spread through Flanders.

324 VIRGIN IN A BLUE CAPE

Pater Damiaanstraat 2
North Bruges ①

A curious statue of the Virgin is attached to a narrow 16th-century corner house in a quiet cobbled street. Protected by a neo-Gothic wooden niche, the Virgin wears a cornflower blue dress as she nonchalantly crushes a snake with her foot.

325 PLAGUE MEMORIAL

Poitevinstraat 2
Historic Centre ①

A shiny tile picture of the Crucifixion catches your eye as you walk down Sint-Jorisstraat. Created in 1900 by the Helman tile factory in Brussels, it replaced a painting of 1866 put up to commemorate a miracle two hundred years earlier when an outbreak of plague was contained.
It was designed by the Bruges artist Henri De Graer.

5 UNUSUAL SMALL MUSEUMS
worth a visit

326 HOLY BLOOD MUSEUM

Burg 13
Historic Centre ②
+32 (0)50 33 67 92
holyblood.com

The neo-Gothic Holy Blood Museum (Museum van het Heilig Bloed) has been dramatically redesigned to show off the glittering church treasures. The highlight is a gold and silver shrine made in 1617 by Bruges goldsmith Jan Crabbe to hold the Holy Blood relic. You can also see a 15th-century crown worn by Mary of Burgundy.

327 FOLKLORE MUSEUM

Balstraat 43
Sint-Anna Quarter ④
+32 (0)50 44 87 43
visitbruges.be

The nostalgic folklore museum (Volksmuseum) occupies a row of eight whitewashed almshouses built in the 17th century as homes for retired shoemakers. The tiny rooms now contain reconstructed interiors including a school-room, pharmacy, grocery store, puppet theatre and an authentic Flemish bar.

327 FOLKLORE MUSEUM

328 ARENTSHUIS

Dijver 16
Historic Centre ②
+32 (0)50 44 87 43
visitbruges.be

Situated in an 18th-century house built over the Dijver canal, the small Arentshuis museum contains a collection of drawings and paintings by Frank Brangwyn, the son of a 19th-century British architect who settled in Bruges. Brangwyn gave 400 of his works to the city 'as a memorial of my love for your great city'.

329 FRIETMUSEUM

Vlamingstraat 33
Historic Centre ①
+32 (0)50 34 01 50
frietmuseum.be

It's one of the world's oddest museums, located in a Gothic building that has been standing since 1399. Where merchants from Genoa once traded, Belgian entrepreneur Eddy Van Belle has created a quirky, cartoonish museum dedicated to the humble Belgian fried potato. Van Belle is also the owner of the chocolate museum as well as the Lumina Domestica museum dedicated to his private collection of old lamps.

330 THE SMALLEST MUSEUM

Driekroezenstraat 19
Begijnhof Quarter ⑤

It's just a window filled with a collection of objects. But the Smallest Museum is one of the oddest spots in Bruges. The owner displays a few items from his eccentric collection of rare Belgian vinyl records, Coca-Cola merchandising, Expo 58 souvenirs and Second World War relics. He occasionally allows visitors inside to see all the other stuff he has gathered over the years.

The 5 most UNEXPECTED PLAQUES

331 **DANTE'S INFERNO**
Academiestraat 1
Historic Centre ①

The Florentine poet Dante is quoted on the wall of a building occupied in the 15th century by merchants from Florence. The verse comes from Dante's *Inferno* where a detail of Hell is compared to a dike built by the Flemings between Bruges and Wissant.

332 **CHARLES FRYATT**
Kazernevest 4
East Bruges ④

You have to search to find the little memorial park next to the law courts. It commemorates twelve Belgians and one British civilian executed here by the Germans in the First World War. The bullet holes have been left in the brick wall as a permanent memorial to the victims, among them Charles Fryatt, captain of the SS Brussels, who was executed for attempting to sink a U-boat.

333 GEORGES RODENBACH

Jan Van Eyckplein 8
Historic Centre ①

You might have expected a statue to Georges Rodenbach, whose novel *Bruges-la-Morte* brought so many tourists to Bruges, but there is almost nothing, just a small hidden bronze plaque on the steps of the house De Rode Steen. It was put up in 1948 by Rodenbach's descendants, although the writer never stayed here.

334 AIR RAID MEMORIAL

Balsemboomstraat
East Bruges ④

A curious war memorial on the side wall of a house has the names and ages of 17 local people killed in a British air raid on the night of 17 October 1917. The bombs were intended to hit a German barracks, but missed their target, destroying 11 houses and killing 17 local people including six members of the Janssens family.

335 CHARLES II OF ENGLAND

Hoogstraat 6
Historic Centre ②

A surprising stone plaque is attached to the side wall of the Casselbergh Hotel. It states that the young British king Charles II lived in exile in this building for three years, along with his two brothers. During his stay, he became an honorary member of the local archers' guild and founded the Grenadier Guards.

The 5 best places to UNDERSTAND BRUGES' HISTORY

336 GRUUTHUSE PALACE
Dijver 17-C
Historic Centre ②
+32 (0)50 44 87 43
visitbruges.be

Bruges has many museums, but not one is dedicated to its history, so you have to work it out for yourself. You might begin with the fabulous palace built by the 15th-century arms dealer Lodewijk van Gruuthuse. Its rooms are filled with furniture, altarpieces, musical instruments, paintings, tapestries and lace. Due to reopen in spring 2019.

337 STADHUIS
Burg 12
Historic Centre ②
+32 (0)50 44 87 43
visitbruges.be

Not many tourists go inside the 14th-century Stadhuis on Burg. But it helps you to understand the history of Bruges if you climb the steps to the great hall on the upper floor. Here you can admire the stunning wood ceiling along with 12 large murals painted in 1895 that offer a romantic history of the city.

338 SINT-JANSHOSPITAAL
Mariastraat 38
Begijnhof Quarter ⑤
+32 (0)50 44 87 43
visitbruges.be

Founded next to a canal in about 1150, the Sint-Janshospitaal is one of the oldest hospitals in the world. Its vast wards were still treating patients in the 1860s, but it is now an engaging museum dedicated to the history of healthcare in Bruges.

339 OUDE BEURSPLEIN

Vlamingstraat 33-35
Historic Centre ①

The world's first rudimentary stock exchange originated in a 13th-century tavern with a sign outside showing three purses. Known as the *beurs*, it attracted foreign merchants from Spain and Italy. By the 15th century, it was one of the great hubs of the mediaeval economy, leading to the word *bourse* for a stock exchange.

340 ADORNES ESTATE

Peperstraat 3
Sint-Anna Quarter ④
+32 (0)50 33 88 83
adornes.org

The little private museum dedicated to the Adornes family is virtually unknown. It opened in 2014 in a row of tiny white almshouses founded by a family that moved to Bruges from Genoa in the 13th century. The main focus is on Anselm Adornes, a leading merchant, diplomat and art patron, who was murdered in Scotland in 1483.

338 SINT-JANSHOSPITAAL

MARY OF BURGUNDY

30 PLACES TO DISCOVER CULTURE

The 5 best places to see
FLEMISH ART

341 **GROENINGEMUSEUM**
Dijver 12
Historic Centre ②
+32 (0)50 44 87 43
visitbruges.be

The Groeningemuseum art collection includes exceptional paintings by Flemish Primitives who worked in Bruges in the 15th century, including Jan van Eyck, Pieter Pourbus and Hans Memling. But it also has an impressive collection of melancholy 19th-century Flemish symbolist paintings along with examples of Marcel Broodthaers' quirky Surrealism.

342 **SINT-JANSHOSPITAAL**
Mariastraat 38
Begijnhof Quarter ⑤
+32 (0)50 44 87 43
visitbruges.be

A little chapel attached to the Sint-Janshospitaal contains a collection of six paintings by the 15th-century artist Hans Memling. Four were painted for the hospital, where Memling spent time as a patient.

343 **SINT-JAKOBSKERK**
Sint-Jakobsplein 1
Historic Centre ①

The Sint-Jakobskerk is full of paintings donated by 15th-century foreign merchants. Sometimes you will find a volunteer guide who can reveal the secret of the twisted baroque columns and show you the hidden switch that lights up the painting of the Legend of Saint Lucy.

344 **CATHEDRAL TREASURY**

Steenstraat
Historic Centre ②
+32 (0)50 33 61 88
sintsalvator.be

The Cathedral Treasury is a strange, forgotten place, open for just a few hours in the afternoon. But it contains some unusual Flemish paintings, along with ancient sculptures, reliquaries and relics. Many of the works were rescued from the old Cathedral on Burg when it was demolished after the French Revolution.

345 **ONZE-LIEVE-VROUW-TER-POTTERIE**

Potterierei 79-B
Sint-Anna Quarter ③
+32 (0)50 44 87 43
visitbruges.be

This quiet, forgotten museum is located in an ancient brick hospital on the Potterierei canal. The old rooms and baroque chapel are crammed with strange objects including a neo-Gothic mausoleum erected in memory of Saint Idesbald, a beautiful 14th-century Madonna and a collection of 17th-century Antwerp mannerist paintings.

342 SINT-JANSHOSPITAAL

5 *inspiring* CULTURAL EXPERIENCES

346 **CACTUS CLUB**
AT: MAGDALENAZAAL
Magdalenastraat 27
Suburbs ⑦
cactusmusic.be

The Cactus Club brings some of the Europe's best rock and pop bands to Bruges. The club currently doesn't have a fixed venue, but often uses the Magdalenazaal in the suburbs. The city plans to build a striking new Cactus concert hall and cafe on the Kanaaleiland, close to the station, but it may take some years.

347 **CARILLON CONCERTS**
Markt 7
Historic Centre ②
carillon-brugge.be

The city employs a bell ringer who climbs to a little room at the top of the Belfry to perform carillon concerts. The 47 bells are rung on three mornings every week and on two evenings in the summer. Sometimes the concert will include an unexpected melody. When David Bowie died in 2016, the bell ringer played *Space Oddity* as a tribute.

348 STADSSCHOUWBURG

Vlamingstraat 29
Historic Centre ①
+32 (0)50 44 30 60
ccbrugge.be

The city theatre has a gorgeous 19th-century neo-renaissance interior most people never see. Inspired by the Paris opera house, it is a flamboyant, glittering space with gilt mouldings, red velvet seats and elegant lamps. The programme includes Flemish theatre and contemporary dance.

349 CINEMA LUMIÈRE

Sint-Jakobsstraat 36
Historic Centre ①
+32 (0)50 34 34 65
lumierecinema.be

Film fans adore this charming arthouse cinema in the heart of Bruges. Owned by an alternative film distribution company, it shows indie movies by international directors in three screening rooms, including an intimate space with just 60 seats. It also has a relaxed cafe where you can meet up after the film.

350 TRIËNNALE

triennalebrugge.be

The city organises a major art festival every three years involving innovative and often radical ideas. Lasting several months, the Triënnale Brugge features artist installations, experimental architecture, exhibitions and encounters. Next event in 2021.

The 5 best places to find
STREET ART

351 **MARY OF BURGUNDY**
Hauwerstraat 3
't Zand Quarter ⑥

You won't find much street art in Bruges, but you can track down a few impressive works created for the street art project Legendz. They include a portrait of Mary of Burgundy by the artist Jeremiah Persyn, who works under the street name Jamz Jamezon. It appeared in 2017 on the side wall of the NH Hotel.

352 **JUNGLE**

352 JUNGLE

Baron Ruzette-laan 260
Suburbs ⑦

Street artist Wietse Hindryckx creates beautiful works in black and white, often featuring Japanese themes and exotic animals. His work *Jungle* was painted in 2017 on the side wall of a house on a busy main road out of town. It shows the artist on a trek through the Cambodian jungle.

353 STROOK

Speelmansrei
't Zand Quarter ⑥
strook.eu

The street artist Stefaan De Crook, who signs his works Strook, has created several works in Bruges using old wood salvaged from demolished buildings. In 2017, he created an installation on the side wall of a building on 't Zand square using brown and green planks rescued from a convent.

354 UNDERPASS MURAL

Ring road underpass
Bargeweg
South Bruges ⑤
stanslabbinck.com

Frank Slabbinck creates joyful, colourful works mixing cartoon art and Surrealism. He was commissioned in 2002 to paint a large mural on a concrete underpass near the bus park. The work combines handwritten messages, cartoon characters and abstract faces. He was assisted by his son Stan, who has gone on to create street art in forgotten corners of Bruges.

355 THREE JAPANESE WOMEN

Baron Ruzette-laan 182
Suburbs ⑦

Local street artist Wietse created two gorgeous works on the back wall of a shop in the suburbs. He portrayed three Oriental women in traditional costumes painted in black and white. They are best seen from the towpath on the west bank of the Bruges to Ghent canal.

The 5 **STRANGEST PAINTINGS** *in Bruges*

356 **SIBYLLA SAMBETHA**
AT: MEMLING MUSEUM
Mariastraat 38
Begijnhof Quarter ⑤
+32 (0)50 44 87 43
visitbruges.be

This strange painting in the Memling Museum takes its title from an Old Testament story in which the Persian Sibyl predicts the coming of Christ. The young woman may in fact have been a daughter of Bruges mayor Willem Moreel and his wife Barbara van Vlaenderbergh.

357 **JUDGEMENT OF CAMBYSES**
AT: GROENINGEMUSEUM
Dijver 12
Historic Centre ②
+32 (0)50 44 87 43
visitbruges.be

No one forgets this horrifying 1498 painting showing a corrupt judge being skinned alive. The victim was modelled upon city official Pieter Lanchals who was tortured and beheaded on Markt following a revolt against Maximilian of Austria.

358 **SAINT NICHOLAS**
AT: GROENINGEMUSEUM
Dijver 12
Historic Centre ②
+32 (0)50 44 87 43
visitbruges.be

A painting of Saint Nicholas by the Master of the Legend of Saint Lucy shows the popular saint dressed as a bishop. The work includes several familiar Bruges sights such as the Minnewater, Onze-Lieve-Vrouwekerk and the Jeruzalemkerk.

359 **JAN VAN EYEWERVE AND JACQUEMYNE BUUCK**

AT: GROENINGEMUSEUM
Dijver 12
Historic Centre ②
+32 (0)50 44 87 43
visitbruges.be

Painted by Pieter Pourbus in 1551, this intriguing double portrait was made when Jan was 29 and his young bride was just 19. Several Bruges sights appear in the painting, including the city crane.

360 **SECRET REFLECTION**

AT: GROENINGEMUSEUM
Dijver 12
Historic Centre ②
+32 (0)50 44 87 43
visitbruges.be

Fernand Khnopff's *Secret Reflection* is a mysterious symbolist work of 1902 showing the side wall of the Sint-Janshospitaal and its reflection in the waters of the canal. The round panel above features the face of a mysterious woman gazing at a mask.

5 of the most inspiring
SMALL GALLERIES

361 **SCHIPPERSKAPEL**
Komvest 38
Sint-Gillis Quarter ③
schipperskapel.be

An abandoned chapel has been turned into a striking gallery of contemporary art. Renamed the Chapel of Awesomeness, the neat white interior, where nuns once prayed, is now used for inspiring exhibitions and the occasional concert.

362 **BLACK SWAN GALLERY**
Langerei 24
Sint-Gillis Quarter ③
+32 (0)475 83 94 72
blackswangallery.be

This new gallery is dedicated to edgy work by emerging artists. Established in 2017, the name was inspired by a black swan that caused panic when it suddenly appeared on the canals in 2014. The gallery aims to serve as a hub for serious contemporary art lovers in Bruges, although it is only open at weekends.

363 **PINSART**
Genthof 21
Historic Centre ①
+32 (0)50 67 50 66
pinsart.be

This contemporary gallery occupies a 16th-century gabled house. It organises interesting exhibitions by emerging Belgian artists in a series of white spaces and a video screening room.

364 44 GALLERY

Genthof 44
Historic Centre ①
+32 (0)489 55 26 63
44gallery.be

Luc Rabaey runs an intimate photography gallery in a bare living room with an ancient tiled floor. He sells unconventional works by contemporary Belgian photographers along with art books and postcards.

365 KOEN BROES

Nieuwe Gentweg 49
Begijnhof Quarter ⑤
+32 (0)50 33 37 74
broes.be

Koen Broes has been around since the early 1980s promoting young, relatively unknown artists. He recently moved into a handsome 18th-century house where he presents a personal choice of prints and graphic art. You find bright, optimistic works propped against a fireplace, resting on balls of string or piled up on a table among art books.

363 **PINSART**

The 5 best FILMS *and* FICTION *set in Bruges*

366 **BRUGES-LA-MORTE**
Wollestraat
Historic Centre ②

Published in Paris in 1892, Georges Rodenbach's fin-de-siècle novel *Bruges-la-Morte* tells the story of an Englishman who settled in Bruges after the death of his wife. While wandering the deserted streets, he falls in love with an actress, but finally murders her in a fit of rage. The novel brought thousands of tourists to Bruges to see for themselves the melancholy dead town.

367 **IN BRUGES**
Park
Astridpark Quarter ②

Released in 2008, the black comedy *In Bruges* was filmed in various locations across the city. It caused something of a sensation because a crime film set in Bruges seemed such a weird concept. It was not particularly flattering, yet everyone, even the tourist office, loved the film's quirky Irish humour.

368 THE WHITE QUEEN

Heilige-Geeststraat
Historic Centre ②

The 2013 British TV series *The White Queen* is set in 15th-century England, but many of its scenes were filmed in Bruges. Locations include the Heilige-Geeststraat (standing for a street in London), the Basilica of the Holy Blood (the Tower of London), the Stadhuis (Westminster Hall) and the B&B Nuit Blanche (a tavern and a bedroom).

369 THE NUN'S STORY

Sint-Annarei 22
Sint-Anna Quarter ④

Fred Zimmerman used several locations in Bruges for his 1959 movie *The Nun's Story*. Starring Audrey Hepburn, the film tells the story of a young nun from Bruges who became a missionary in the Belgian Congo. Some key scenes were filmed in a beautiful rococo mansion on Sint-Annarei.

370 PK

Minnewaterpark
South Bruges ⑤

The hugely successful Bollywood romance *PK* was partly filmed in Bruges in 2014. The blockbuster movie features scenes shot in the Minnewater Park, the Markt and on several canals. "We found the innocence and charm we were looking for in Belgium," the director said.

VIEW FROM NUIT BLANCHE

30 PLACES TO STAY

The 5 best

CANALSIDE LODGINGS

371 **CANAL DELUXE**
Moerstraat 24
Historic Centre ①
+32 (0)475 46 67 22
canaldeluxe.com

This is a gorgeous hideaway in a 17th-century almshouse overlooking a quiet canal. You reach it down a tiny hidden lane opposite the Sint-Jakobskerk. The four rooms have unexpected features including oak beams, antique chests and a blazing fire. Owners Tina and Maria provide helpful hints on where to eat along with little extras like homemade cake.

372 **BONIFACIUS**
Groeninge 4
Historic Centre ②
+32 (0)50 49 00 49
bonifacius.be

This guesthouse occupies a sublime waterfront location near the Gruuthuse palace. Once used as a coach house, the 16th-century building has been tastefully decorated with antiques and rich fabrics to create the warm mood of an old Bruges mansion.

373 **HOTEL DE ORANGERIE**
Kartuizerinnen-straat 10
Historic Centre ②
+32 (0)50 34 16 49
hotelorangerie.com

Located in a former 15th-century convent, this luxurious hotel has a waterside terrace overlooking the Dijver canal. The 20 rooms are individually decorated in romantic baroque style by Antwerp interior designer Pieter Porters, while the bar is warmed in winter by a blazing fire.

374 THE PAND HOTEL

Pandreitje 16
Historic Centre ②
+32 (0)50 34 06 66
pandhotel.com

A former 18th-century carriage house on a leafy square near the Dijver has been converted into an elegant 23-room hotel. The bedrooms are furnished with Ralph Lauren fabrics, antiques and paintings. Guest can also enjoy a library with a blazing fire on winter days and an attractive breakfast room filled in the morning with the smell of freshly-baked bread.

375 TER DUINEN

Langerei 52
Sint-Gillis Quarter ③
+32 (0)50.33.04.37
terduinenhotel.be

This is a small waterfront hotel in an 18th-century house near the Potterie museum. The guest rooms are small, but elegant. Some have views of the Langerei canal. The owners are friendly and offer bicycles to tour the town or head off down the canal to Damme.

5 of the most stunning hotels in
HISTORIC BUILDINGS

376 **GRAND HOTEL CASSELBERGH**
Hoogstraat 6
Historic Centre ①
+32 (0)50 44 65 00
grandhotel casselbergh.com

This grand hotel near Burg is located in a row of three restored historic buildings. The interior incorporates old stone columns, an elegant bar and a wellness centre in the vaulted mediaeval basements. Some guest rooms are located in the ancient buildings, while others occupy a bold modern extension designed in 2010 by Brussels architects Buro II (now B2Ai).

376 GRAND HOTEL CASSELBERGH

377 HOTEL NAVARRA

Sint-Jakobsstraat 41
Historic Centre ①
+32 (0)50 34 05 61
hotelnavarra.com

This handsome town house was built in the early 17th century by Juan de Peralta, consul of Navarre. The beautiful rococo entrance leads into a stylish hotel that has kept much of its original grandeur.

378 HOTEL DUKES' PALACE

Prinsenhof 8
Historic Centre ②
+32 (0)50 44 78 88
hoteldukespalace.com

This new luxury hotel occupies a neo-Gothic girls' school built on the site of the 15th-century ducal palace. A nearby hotel had already claimed the name Prinsenhof, so the new arrival had to settle for Dukes' Palace. The only truly grand hotel in Bruges, with underground parking and a spa, it manages to remain low key and often surprisingly affordable.

379 HOTEL BOTERHUIS

Sint-Jakobsstraat 40
Historic Centre ①
+32 (0)50 34 15 11
boterhuis.be

A relaxed family-run hotel located in a 16th-century building with a distinctive round tower. It takes its name from a vanished building where butter was sold. Decorated in traditional Flemish style, the 16 guest rooms incorporate old details like oak beams, but also modern features such as air conditioning.

380 MONSIEUR ERNEST

Wulfhagestraat 43
Historic Centre ⑥
+32 (0)50 96 09 66
monsieurernest.com

Eva Vandewalle and her brother have created a relaxed contemporary hotel where guests are encouraged to meet up in the bar. The hotel occupies a former 19th-century brewery next to a bridge over the lovely Speelmansrei canal.

The 5 finest

ROOMS WITH A VIEW

381 **1669 B&B, THE LOFT**
Sint-Salvators-
kerkhof 16
Historic Centre ②
+32 (0)471 79 57 03
1669.be

This handsome B&B occupies a brick house from 1669 once owned by an antique dealer. There are four rooms in different styles including a romantic attic hideaway named The Loft. This luxurious space is decorated with oiled wood floors, lime walls, exposed beams and a vintage bathtub. The window behind the bed has a stunning view of the old town.

382 **A ROOM WITH A VIEW, LOFT SANTAL**
Hugo Verriest-
straat 10
Sint-Anna Quarter ④
+32 (0)50 33 47 36
aroomwithaview.be

This B&B occupies a gabled house in a quiet street with front gardens that look almost English. It has three rooms decorated in a muted contemporary style, including the attic room Loft Santal. This romantic retreat looks across tiled roofs and gardens to a windmill on the former ramparts.

383 **BOURGOENSCH HOF, ROOM 20**

Wollestraat 35
Historic Centre ②
+32 (0)50 33 16 45
hotelbh.be

This comfortable hotel is located in a former brewery overlooking the pretty Rozenhoedkaai. The rooms come in different sizes with odd details like sloping roofs. You pay a little extra for one of the rooms with a view of the canal. The best is probably number 20 which looks down on the town hall and its hidden back garden where the mayor hosts visitors.

384 **HOTEL ADORNES, ROOM 17**

Sint-Annarei 26
Sint-Anna Quarter ④
+32 (0)50 34 13 36
adornes.be

The Hotel Adornes occupies a stylishly renovated row of three brick gable houses on a quiet canal. Some bedrooms have oak beams, while those at the front have views of the canal. Our favourite is number 17 which has a stunning view looking east. Free bicycles are available to explore the city.

385 **MAISON AMODIO, KNOKKE-LE-ZOUTE ROOM**

Molenmeers 22
Sint-Anna Quarter ④
+32 (0)468 35 96 40
maisonamodio.eu

Geert and Henri have created a beautiful B&B in a 16th-century house near the centre. It has three guest rooms decorated with little details evoking travel destinations. For a spectacular view of the old town, book the Knokke Room in the attic. Guests also have the use of a spacious living room lined with bookcases and an airy breakfast room overlooking a courtyard garden.

The 5 most
ROMANTIC B&BS

386 **CASA ROMANTICO**
Eekhoutstraat 37
Astridpark Quarter ②
+32 (0)50 67 80 93
www.casa-romantico.be

This is, as the name says, a romantic house. Hidden down a quiet street in the heart of Bruges, the interior is decorated in New England beach house style with pale wood floors, white furniture and antique bathtubs. It also has a heated swimming pool in the back garden to add a final touch of luxury.

387 **NUIT BLANCHE**
Groeninge 2
Historic Centre ②
+32 (0)494 40 04 47
bb-nuitblanche.com

The artist David de Graef has created a fabulous guest house in a historic Bruges house. The Belgian royal couple Albert and Paola stayed here after they married in 1959. The two guest rooms look out on a mediaeval walled garden and a little canal. They are designed in the style of a Jan van Eyck painting with old stone fireplaces, stained glass windows and huge oak beds.

388 NUMBER 11

Peerdenstraat 11
Historic Centre ①
+32 (0)50 33 06 75
number11.be

This is an exceptional guest house hidden down a quiet cobbled lane near Burg. It has just four guest rooms decorated in different styles, along with an intimate pine-panelled lounge heated by a log-burning stove and a walled back garden filled with birdsong.

389 LA SUITE SANS CRAVATE

Langestraat 126
Sint-Anna Quarter ④
+32 (0)50 67 83 10
lasuite-bb.com

Veronique and Henk have created a gorgeous place to stay in a 17th-century brick building opposite their restaurant Sans Cravate. The three guest rooms (named after grape varieties) are decorated in a tasteful, rustic style, with quirky details dotted around. Ask for the Savignon Blanc Suite to sleep in a stunning romantic hideaway under the roof beams.

390 MAISON LE DRAGON

Eekhoutstraat 5
Historic Centre ②
+32 (0)50 72 06 54
maisonledragon.be

This romantic guest house is located in a 16th-century house with stylish interiors. The decoration includes wood panelling, rococo antiques and ornate mirrors. It also has a walled garden and a lounge with an open fire for chilly northern days.

5 *striking*

B&B INTERIORS

391 **KIND OF OJ**
Guido Gezellelaan 36
't Zand ⑥
+32 (0)498 56 17 15
kindofoj.com

Jo Hoeven has turned a 19th-century family home into a stunning B&B filled with Dutch design objects and contemporary art. The three spacious suites are decorated in a quirky, unique style with bold fabrics, stacks of books and exotic plants, while the bathtubs are made out of baked clay.

391 KIND OF OJ

392 FORT LAPIN

Fort Lapin 25
Suburbs ⑦
+32 (0)477 22 32 16
fortlapin.be

An impressive neo-baroque corner house overlooking the old harbour has been lovingly renovated to create a unique B&B. The five rooms are furnished with comfortable beds, wood beams and odd antiques. It's worth trying to book Kamer Louise in the turret which has a separate upstairs bedroom.

393 ZAKSKE13

Zakske 13
Historic Centre ①
+32 (0)50 67 73 99
zakske13.be

This stylish B&B is located in an old factory at the end of a narrow Bruges *zakske* (alleyway). It's an interesting, quiet location just off Ezelstraat. The guest rooms are decorated in a clean modern style with wood floors, boldly coloured walls and designer lamps.

394 DE WALVISCH

Predikherenrei 23
East Bruges ④
+32 (0)476 77 61 47
walvisch.be

This beautiful B&B occupies a 1906 brick building on the Coupure canal. Originally a cafe, its name comes from a stone above the entrance carved with a whale. The owners carefully restored the building in 2018 in a quiet contemporary style while preserving original elements, including the old cafe sign.

395 4B B&B

Genthof 26
Historic Centre ①
+32 (0)50 34 74 45
4bbrugge.be

A stylish urban guest house with a striking rusted steel façade in the heart of the old town. The interior is decorated with contemporary art, bright cushions and plants. Ella lays out a delicious home-made breakfast based on local produce such as veal meatloaf from her local butcher and goat's cheese from Damme.

The 5 best

BUDGET SLEEPS

396 **HOTEL NOTRE DAME**
Mariastraat 8
Historic Centre ②
+32 (0)50 33 31 93
hotelnotredame.be

Located in a white neoclassical building, this traditional hotel has some of the lowest prices in town. The owners have upgraded the bedrooms while preserving the historical feel of the building. Some rooms are quite small and the stairs are steep, but this could be the perfect spot for a young couple who just need a comfortable place to sleep.

397 **BAERT – BED AND BREAKFAST**
Westmeers 28
't Zand Quarter ⑥
+32 (0)50 33 05 30
bedandbreakfast brugge.be

Huub Baert runs a charming little B&B in a whitewashed building once used as stables. He has just two bright rooms with secluded terraces on a little canal where you can catch the afternoon sun. Baert make a big effort to take care of his guests, from providing a parking space in his garage to offering tips on where to eat.

398 **HOTEL GROENINGHE**
Korte Vulders-straat 29
't Zand Quarter ⑥
+32 (0)50 34 32 55
hotelgroeninghe.be

Located in a quiet cobbled lane, this family-run hotel occupies an old town house dating from 1858. You have to accept the creaky floorboards and steep stairs. But the rooms are comfortable for the price you pay.

399 **HOTEL GOEZEPUT**

Goezeputstraat 29
't Zand Quarter ⑥
+32 (0)50 34 26 94
hotelgoezeput.be

Karel and Bénédicte recently renovated a 19th-century convent to create a stylish little hotel in a quiet corner of town. The guest rooms are sometimes small, but they are attractively designed, with contemporary showers, wood floors and oak beams. It's worth asking for one of the quiet loft rooms for the view over the rooftops.

400 **SNUFFEL**

Ezelstraat 42
North Bruges ③
+32 (0)50 33 31 33
snuffel.one

This cool, contemporary hostel was rebuilt in 2015 by Bruges firm Salens Architecten and decorated with poems cut in rusted steel plates by sculptor Maud Bekaert. With a cafe, courtyard and concert space, it's a friendly, inspiring place to meet up with other travellers. Rooms range from six-person dorms to simple doubles.

400 SNUFFEL

DAMSE VAART

50 ACTIVITIES FOR THE WEEKEND – IN AND OUTSIDE BRUGES

The 5 best

URBAN WALKS

401 RAMPARTS
BEGIN AT:
Ezelpoort
Ezelstraat
North Bruges ③

Landscaped in the 19th century, the ramparts form an attractive green belt around the old town. You can wander along meandering paths leading to ancient city gates, climb up to windmills and drop into neighbourhood cafes along the way. Not many tourists come out here, so you find yourself among local people walking their dogs and kids riding their bikes to school. The total circuit is just over 7 km, almost all on quiet paths.

401 RAMPARTS

402 HIDDEN CANALS

BEGIN AT:
Speelmansrei
't Zand Quarter ⑥

Some canals in Bruges are crowded, but others are often deserted. Begin on the quiet Speelmansrei, following the canal until you come to a small bridge. Now turn down Moerstraat to pick up the canal again at the Ezelstraat.

403 THE MERCHANTS' QUARTER

BEGIN AT:
Vlamingstraat 35
Historic Centre ①

Not many tourists walk through the quarter where foreign merchants settled in the 15th century. You can wander down quiet lanes overlooked by tall Gothic houses and across squares where foreign traders once sold silks, spices, beer and furs. Begin on the square in front of the former stock exchange at Vlamingstraat 35.

404 FORGOTTEN BRUGES

BEGIN AT:
't Zand
't Zand Quarter ⑥

A quiet, forgotten corner of Bruges lies beyond 't Zand square. Here you find small almshouses, intimate restaurants and local shops. Head down Boeveriestraat to reach the ramparts and then follow the meandering path to the right to reach the Smedenpoort. Now turn right down Smedenstraat.

405 CANALS BY NIGHT

BEGIN AT:
Meestraat
Historic Centre ②

You can put together a canal walk once the crowds have gone to take in romantic spots after dark. First walk down Meestraat to reach an ancient bridge which is one of the loveliest (and quietest) spots on the canals. Now navigate your way along the canals Groenerei, Predikherenrei, Verwersdijk and Spinolarei.

The 5 best

BIKE RENTALS *and* TOURS

406 **DE KETTING**
Gentpoortstraat 23
South Bruges ⑤
+32 (0)50 34 41 96
deketting.be

De Ketting (The Chain) is a friendly bike shop where you can rent a sturdy Belgian bike to cycle out of town to Damme, Sluis or even the coast. They will also fix a baby seat on the back or rent you an electric bike for the day. The rates are the cheapest in Bruges.

407 **BRUGES BIKE RENTAL**
Niklaas Despars-straat 17
Historic Centre ①
+32 (0)50 61 61 08
brugesbikerental.be

A helpful bike shop in a quiet lane just north of Markt. Located in a cellar below a hairdresser's, the shop rents bikes for half a day or longer. They also stock tandems and smart electric bikes. Cheaper than other places, but their bikes are sometimes older models.

408 PINK BEAR BIKE TOURS

MEET AT:
Markt
Historic Centre ②
+32 (0)50 61 66 86
pinkbear.be

Mieke organises bike tours along the canal from Bruges to Damme. She is a relaxed, friendly guide who points out unexpected details like storks on chimney pots and lambs playing in meadows.

409 FIETSKOETSEN BRUGGE

Burg
Historic Centre ②
+32 (0)478 40 95 57
fietskoetsenbrugge.be

Pieter Jacques launched rickshaw tours in Bruges after a visit to Manhattan. He now has a team of energetic young guides who pedal tourists around quiet cobbled streets in Polish-built rickshaws with space for two (or three at a squeeze). The 30-minute tours are done in Dutch, English, French or Spanish.

410 BLUE BIKES

Bruges station
South Bruges ⑤
blue-bike.be

The Blue Bike system lets you rent bikes at a railway station for a modest fee. But first you have to become a member, so it only works if you are in Belgium for a longer period. You join by filling in a simple online form and paying a small annual fee. You then receive a smartcard through the post which you can use at any Blue Bike station to release up to two bikes. The station in Bruges has over 50 bikes available.

5 *great places to*
TAKE CHILDREN

411 **HISTORIUM**
Markt 1
Historic Centre ②
+32 (0)50 27 03 11
historium.be

You might enjoy the Historium. Or at least your kids might. Designed by a team of professional historians, it sets out to tell the story of 15th-century Bruges in a series of seven rooms decorated like film sets. You can look inside Jan van Eyck's studio, walk through the harbour and experience the smell of a brothel.

412 **GRAAF VISARTPARK**
Karel de Stoutelaan 10
Suburbs ⑦

King Leopold II created this formal park just outside the old town in the early 20th century. It now has an adventure playground that is perfect for kids who need to burn off some energy. You can usually find a pop-up bar in the summer months under the old trees.

413 **MISSION MICHELANGELO**
Ezelstraat 79
North Bruges ③
+32 (0)472 91 16 11
amazingescape.be

The escape room Mission Michelangelo is a fun way to spend a rainy day in Bruges. Inspired by the theft of Michaelangelo's Bruges Madonna, players hunt for clues in well-made historical interiors. Your team has 60 minutes to save the priceless masterpiece from destruction.

414 BELFORT

Markt 7
Historic Centre ②
+32 (0)50 44 87 43
museabrugge.be

It's 366 steps to the top of the belfry tower. Not for everyone, but perfect for young children with energy to burn. On the way up, they can admire the fortified treasury, the massive nine-ton mechanical carillon and the wood-panelled room where the town carilloneur plays. The view from the top is worth all the effort.

415 DE ZEVEN TORENTJES

Canadaring 41
Suburbs ⑦
+32 (0)50 35 40 43
kiboe.be

This children's farm just south of Bruges is the perfect spot for a day out with young children. Kids can explore several farm buildings including a cow shed, pig sty and bakery (with a wood fire). They can also scramble on wooden horses in the playground and eat a pancake in the cafe.

415 DE ZEVEN TORENTJES

The 5 best
SMALL FESTIVALS

416 **CACTUS**
Minnewaterpark
South Bruges ⑤
+32 (0)50 33 20 14
cactusfestival.be

This relaxed music festival is held every summer in the magical setting of the Minnewater Park. It's a friendly, intimate event spread over three days featuring an eclectic mix of international rock bands and solo singers.

417 **BENENWERK**
Astridpark and other locations
Historic Centre
benenwerk.be

A huge dance marathon takes over ten open spaces in Bruges for one summer night in August. Beginning in the early evening, the festival features live bands and DJs performing various dance styles including swing, tango, salsa, electro and dubstep. No entry charge. Just turn up and dance.

417 **BENENWERK**

418 **KLINKENDE KROEGEN**

HELD ON:

Wednesday evenings
July-August
brugge.be/klinkende-kroegen-5

A modest summer event for music fans and tourists featuring local bands performing in the city's most relaxed cafes, bars and bistros. The programme takes in just about every music style, including blues, jazz, eighties, funk and soul.

419 **MAFESTIVAL**

AT: CONCERTGEBOUW

't Zand 34
't Zand Quarter ⑥
+32 (0)50 33 22 83
www.mafestival.be

It used to be called Musica Antique. Now it's just MA. Held in various venues across the old town including the stunning Concertgebouw, this ten-day festival brings together dedicated musicians who perform early European music on authentic historical instruments. The festival also features an instrument makers' fair, along with organised bike rides to outdoor locations where musicians perform short concerts.

420 **MOODS!**

Burg
Historic Centre ②
+32 (0)50 33 20 14
moodsbrugge.be

The Moods! summer festival brings international bands and solo performers to the beautiful Burg square in the heart of the city. The open-air concerts take place over several evenings in late July and early August on a stage set up against the stunning backdrop of the floodlit Gothic town hall.

5 interesting

HISTORIC PROCESSIONS

421 **HOLY BLOOD PROCESSION**
LEAVES FROM:
Smedenpoort (Dijver during works)
't Zand Quarter ⑥
bloedprocessiebrugge.be

Held every year on Ascension Day since about 1291, the Holy Blood Procession involves a precious relic said to contain drops of Christ's blood. Some 1500 local people parade through the streets in a procession stretching for more than a kilometre.

422 **BLINDEKENS PROCESSION**
LEAVES FROM:
Blindekens Chapel
Kreupelenstraat
't Zand Quarter ⑥
brugsebelofte.be

For more than 700 years, members of the Order of Our Lady of Blindekens have set off on 15 August from the little Blindekens chapel. Dressed in long blue robes and caps, they keep alive a tradition begun in 1304 after the Battle of Pevelenberg, when local women promised to offer a candle every year "until the end of time" if their men returned safely.

423 STERRENSTOET

LEAVES FROM:
Sint-Janshospitaal
Mariastraat
Begijnhof Quarter ⑤
comitevoorinitiatief.be/brugge/sterrenstoet

It looks like another mediaeval procession, but the Sterrenstoet only began in 1932. Held a few days before Christmas to raise money for the poor, it recreates the story of the Christmas star. More than 100 people take part dressed in historical costumes, along with drummers and a flock of sheep.

424 THE GOLDEN TREE / PRAALSTOET VAN DE GOUDEN BOOM

visit-bruges.be

Once every five years, a spectacular procession is organised to commemorate the wedding in 1468 of Charles the Bold and Margaret of York. It involves thousands of people dressed in historical costumes, along with musicians, jugglers and even animals. The next procession will be held in 2022.

425 MEIFOOR

't Zand
't Zand Quarter ⑥
brugge.be/meifoor

The Meifoor has been held more than 800 times since it began in 1200. Originally an annual commercial fair, it has gradually evolved into a funfair that sprawls across several squares for three weeks. Running from late April to early May, it features rides, stands selling *smoutebollen* (fritters), processions and fireworks.

The 5 best
BEACH TOWNS
near Bruges

426 **ZEEBRUGGE**
Hinterland ⑧
brugge.be/zeebrugge

It's mainly known as a seaport, but Zeebrugge is also a modest beach town. You can wander along the broad sand, eat fresh fish in the old harbour quarter and observe the port from a high observation deck. When the wind is strong, kids fly kites on the beach while more serious kite surfers ride the waves. Trains from Bruges take 18 minutes.

427 **BLANKENBERGE**
Hinterland ⑧
blankenberge.be

Blankenberge used to be a depressed place, but it has recently made a serious comeback. You might be surprised to find art nouveau houses, hip beach bars and cool B&Bs, along with Belgium's only pier. Trains from Bruges take just 13 minutes.

427 **BLANKENBERGE**

429 **DE HAAN**

428 **OSTEND**
Hinterland ⑧
visitoostende.be

Ostend no longer calls itself "The Queen of the Belgian Resorts," yet this faded beach town still has a hint of grandeur as well as a vibrant cultural life. You find good fish restaurants in the old town, as well as excellent museums, cafes, and shops. Trains take 14 minutes from Bruges.

429 **DE HAAN**
Hinterland ⑧
visitdehaan.be

De Haan has hardly changed since it was laid out in 19th-century German romantic style. The strict planning laws laid down at the time have prevented the construction of modern apartment buildings, and you still find small family-run hotels, unique B&Bs and modest restaurants. Take the train to Ostend and then ride the coast tram to De Haan's beautiful art nouveau tram station.

430 **KNOKKE**
Hinterland ⑧
knokke-heist.info

Knokke is an exclusive resort where rich northern Europeans spend their weekends. Developed in the 19th century by the Lippens family, it is dominated by high fashion and exclusive brands that make the town rather soulless, but it has attractive quarters behind the beach along with art galleries and cafes. The train from Bruges takes 20 minutes.

5 *of the best places to*
EAT AROUND BRUGES

431 **SIPHON**
Damse Vaart-Oost 1
Damme
Hinterland ⑧
+32 (0)50 62 02 02
siphon.be

This family-run restaurant occupies a farmhouse next to the canal in Damme. Locals have been coming here for years to eat regional specialities, including meat grilled over an open fire, Zeebrugge shrimps and fresh eel. You can also drink a Siphon craft beer made in a microbrewery installed in an old barn.

432 **DE LAMME GOEDZAK**
Kerkstraat 13
Damme
Hinterland ⑧
+32 (0)472 84 79 72
delammegoedzak.be

This family-run restaurant is located in an old Damme house with a tiled floor, heavy curtains and rustic details. The menu offers typical regional cooking including steaks, Zeeland mussels and sole. They fry their chips once in oil and a second time in beef dripping to create the perfect Flemish *frietjes*.

433 **'T WERFTJE**
Werfkaai 29
Zeebrugge
Hinterland ⑧
+32 (0)497 55 30 10
twerftje.be

Mike and Herlinde run an old cafe on the harbour front in Zeebrugge that has been around for more than a century. It's a plain, friendly place with wood-panelling and mirrors, where local fishermen drop by for a bowl of fish soup or Herlinde's famous *garnaalkroketten*.

434 **OESTERPUT**
Wenduinse Steenweg 16
Blankenberge
Hinterland ⑧
+32 (0)50 41 10 35
oesterput.com

No booking. Nothing fancy. Just perfect seafood. The Devriendt family's restaurant is hidden in the dunes near the marina. It looks quite basic, but they serve some of the best seafood on the coast, including dripping wet oysters, little whelks extracted from the shell with a pin and freshly-cooked lobsters kept alive in large tanks.

435 **BRASSERIE FORT VAN BEIEREN**
Gemeneweide-straat 51
Koolkerke
Hinterland ⑧
+32 (0)50 67 95 86
hippo.be/fort

You can eat lunch in an old white farmhouse located next to the 18th-century Fort van Beieren. The kitchen serves simple food along with a few specialities like grilled scampi. Or you can just sit outside on the terrace with a Brugse Zot beer. It's a 20-minute cycle ride from town.

434 OESTERPUT

The 5 best
BIKE ROUTES
out of town

436 **BRUGES TO DAMME**
BEGIN AT:
Dampoort
Sint-Gillis Quarter ⑦
fietsnet.be

This beautiful route follows the wide Damse Vaart canal built by Napoleon in the early 19th century. The 30-minute ride to Damme takes you along a quiet rural road shaded by tall Canadian poplars. From Damme, you can continue along the canal to the Dutch border town of Sluis. Follow the *fietsnet* cycle network numbers 23, 60, 10 and 6 to reach Damme.

437 **BRUGES TO GHENT CANAL**
BEGIN AT:
Katelijnepoort
South Bruges ⑤
fietsnet.be

It's possible to follow the canal towpath all the way from Bruges to Ghent, a distance of 45 km. But you can also do a shorter ride from Bruges to Beernem, just 14 km away. You begin at the Katelijnepoort, where the cycle route goes under the ring road to reach the canal. Now follow the *fietsnet* numbered signs 5, 69, 71, 87, 88 to arrive in Beernem.

438 BRUGES TO BLANKENBERGE

BEGIN AT:
Kolenkaai
Suburbs ⑦
fietsnet.be

You can cycle to Blankenberge in about 70 minutes if the wind is not against you. Most of the time, you are crossing flat Flemish farmland, but the final stretch takes you through the wild nature reserve of Uitkerkse Polder. Start at cycle point 27 on the ramparts, followed by 31, 69, 78, 88, 40, 96, 30 26, 76. Pause in the pretty village of Lissewege for a coffee.

439 GROENE GORDEL

BEGIN AT:
Kolenkaai
Suburbs ⑦
groenegordelbrugge.be

The Groene Gordel (Green Ring) route takes you right out into the countryside around Bruges. The signposted 53-km route has been carefully put together to take in forests, castles, quiet canals and attractive villages. The Groene Gordel website includes a useful map of the route.

440 TILLEGEM WOODS

BEGIN AT:
Smedenpoort
't Zand Quarter ⑥
fietsnet.be

Leave town by the Smedenpoort to explore the woods just west of Bruges. After passing through the Sint-Michiels suburbs, you can follow a meandering route past wayside chapels, farms with honey for sale and impressive country houses. Follow numbered signs 46, 57, 70, 59, 99, 97 and 13 to reach the romantic Loppem castle.

The 5 most interesting
HISTORIC PLACES
around Bruges

441 **CENTRALE BEGRAAFPLAATS**
Kleine Kerkhofstraat
Assebroek
Suburbs ⑦

The city cemetery is a quiet, romantic graveyard filled with crumbling stone tombs of eminent locals like poet Guido Gezelle and sculptor Henri Pickery. Look out for the strange tomb of Antoine Michel Wernaer, known to the grave diggers as Pirate Piet (with an ivy-covered stone skull on top) and the English cemetery hidden away in an overgrown corner.

442 **DAMME**
Hinterland ⑧
visitdamme.be

Once a busy seaport, Damme was fortified in the 16th century and revived in recent years as a book town. It's a pretty little place where you can wander through quiet cobbled streets, follow a walking trail and squeeze into the smallest bookshop in the Low Countries.

443 **FORT VAN BEIEREN**
Kasteeldreef 21
Koolkerke
Hinterland ⑧

The Fort van Beieren is a curious relic of the wars fought in this region in the early 18th century. The fort was constructed in 1705 by French troops fighting in the Spanish War of Succession. It was torn down in 1956, leaving just the vague outline of the earth ramparts.

444 SEAFRONT ZEEBRUGGE

Vismijnstraat 7
Zeebrugge
Hinterland ⑧
+32 (0)50 55 14 15
seafront.be

The huge industrial sheds in Zeebrugge where fish used to be auctioned have been turned into a maritime theme park. The main attraction is a former Soviet submarine from the Cold War era where you can crawl through claustrophobic compartments past narrow bunk beds while hidden speakers play patriotic Russian songs.

445 LOPPEM CASTLE

Steenbrugsestraat 26
Zedelgem-Loppem
Hinterland ⑧
+32 (0)50 82 22 45
kasteelvanloppem.be

Located in the countryside just outside Bruges, Loppem Castle is not too well known. You can sometimes be the only visitor. Yet this 19th-century Flemish neo-Gothic castle designed by the architect Jean de Bethune has a fascinating interior. The castle also has a maze planted in 1873 at the far end of the estate.

441 CENTRALE BEGRAAFPLAATS

The 5 best **WALKS** *near Bruges*

446 LAPPERSFORTBOS
BEGIN AT:
Vaartdijkstraat
Suburbs ⑦

Local activists campaigned hard to save the tiny woodland area outside Bruges known as the Lappersfortbos. Squeezed between a railway line, a canal and an industrial zone, this little wood is an unexpected, romantic spot with meandering trails, a stream and a playground.

447 KASTEELBOSSEN
BEGIN AT:
DOMEIN TILLEGEM
Wittemolenstraat
Suburbs ⑦

An extensive area of wild woodland called Kasteelbossen (Castle Woods) lies just west of Bruges. It incorporates the estates of three historic castles built by wealthy Bruges families. The Drie Kastelenwandelroute (Three Castles Trail) takes you on a 12-km circular ramble through this interesting landscape of meadows, woods and orchards.

448 ASSEBROEKSE MEERSEN

BEGIN AT:
ASSEBROEK CHURCH
Pastoor Verhaegheplein
Assebroek
Hinterland ⑧

This wild and windswept area of meadows and marshland lies just south of Bruges. The land is marked by three mysterious concentric circles invisible on the ground but clearly visible on Google Earth. You can walk along tracks lined with pollarded willow trees and spot rare migrating birds. But it can be a bleak spot in winter.

449 THE COAST WALK

kustwandelroute.be

It's possible to hike the entire length of the Belgian coast following the marked trails of the *kustwandelroute* (coastal walking route). The best stretch runs through dunes planted with pine trees in the 19th century between De Haan and Wenduine. But you can pick up the trail at any point and walk as far as you want, since the coast tram stops all along the route.

450 HET ZWIN

Graaf Léon Lippensdreef 8
Knokke-Heist
Hinterland ⑧
+32 (0)50 60 70 86
zwin.be

The Zwin is a wild area of marshland and dunes to the east of Knokke. You can set off on foot on marked trails, looking out for nesting storks and even grazing Highland cattle. There are several marked trails across this empty landscape ranging from 2 km to 12 km.

SIMON STEVIN

20 PEOPLE WHO MADE BRUGES

The 5 most inspiring **ARTISTS** *and* **WRITERS** *from Bruges*

451 **FERNAND KHNOPFF**
Langestraat 1
Sint-Anna Quarter ④

The artist Fernand Khnopff spent his childhood in the elegant waterfront house at Langestraat 1, now the Hotel ter Reien. Khnopff rarely returned to his birthplace, afraid the city would lose its spell if he spent too long there. But almost all of his paintings are haunted by his childhood memories of this house rising out of the dark water.

452 **HUGO CLAUS**

Born in 1929 in the Sint-Janshospitaal, the Flemish writer Hugo Claus spent his youth in a boarding school run by nuns. He became an acclaimed poet, painter and writer, nominated many times for the Nobel Prize in Literature. His novel *The Sorrow of Belgium* dealt with collaboration during World War II.

453 PIETER ASPE

De Loge
Sint-Jakobsstraat 6
Historic Centre ①
+32 (0)50 61 13 66
aspenv.be

The Flemish writer Pieter Aspe worked for many years as a caretaker in the Holy Blood Chapel before he became a crime writer. Most of his books are set in Bruges and the surrounding countryside. He recently opened a bookstore and gallery along with the Bruges cartoonist Marec. Try his thriller *From Bruges with Love*.

454 SAMMY SLABBINCK

sammyslabbinck.be

The son of Bruges artist Frank Slabbinck, Sammy Slabbinck spent his teenage years hunting through flea markets in search of old magazines. He now has a vast collection ranging from *Paris Match* to *Playboy* stored in his attic. He uses them to create surreal collages blending incongruous magazine fragments.

455 ROBERT DEVRIENDT

robertdevriendt.be

Born in 1955, the Bruges artist Robert Devriendt is often compared to Flemish Primitives like Jan van Eyck and Hans Memling. But he doesn't see it that way. He paints sequences of tiny works in astonishing detail. Like enigmatic unfinished movies, they illustrate dark themes like lust or murder.

5 *famous* FOREIGNERS IN BRUGES

456 **GIOVANNI ARNOLFINI**

The young Italian Giovanni Arnolfini arrived in Bruges in 1420 to work as a merchant and banker. In 1434 he found himself a wife, Giovanna Cenami, born into a rich family from his home town of Lucca. The famous Van Eyck painting in London's National Gallery is believed to be a wedding portrait of Arnolfini and his wife, painted in their home in Bruges.

457 **WILLIAM CAXTON**

The English merchant William Caxton lived in Bruges for many years. He led the English Nation for eight years, set up a printing press in partnership with the local printer Collaert Mansion, and printed the first book in English in Bruges in 1475.

458 JUAN LUIS VIVES

Bonifaciusbrug
Historic Centre ②

Hidden in the trees near the little Bonifacius bridge, the bronze bust of Juan Luis Vives doesn't attract much attention. It was created by the Spanish sculptor Ramón Mateu in 1957 in memory of a 16th-century Spanish humanist who settled in Bruges in 1512.

459 TOMMASO PORTINARI

Garenmarkt 15
Astridpark Quarter ②

The 15th-century Italian merchant Tommaso Portinari represented the Medici bank in Bruges. He commissioned Memling to paint a portrait of himself and his wife, now in New York's Metropolitan Museum of Art. The College of Europe occupies the 18th-century Hotel Portinari, on the site of the Italian merchant's palace.

460 FANNY TROLLOPE

Het Witte Huis
Gistelsesteenweg 30
Suburbs ⑦

The British writer Fanny Trollope moved to Bruges in 1832 with her bankrupt husband and children, including the young Anthony Trollope. Desperately poor, the family rented a large white villa named Château d'Hondt, just outside the town. Her husband and son are buried in a corner of the municipal cemetery known as the *Engels kerkhof* (English cemetery).

The 5 most

REMARKABLE TOMBS

461 **MARY OF BURGUNDY**
AT: ONZE-LIEVE-VROUWEKERK
Mariastraat
Historic Centre ②
+32 (0)50 44 87 11
visitbruges.be

Mary of Burgundy, daughter of Charles the Bold, died in 1482 when she fell from her horse in the woods near Bruges. Her husband Maximilian commissioned a spectacular tomb in 1495 to stand in the Onze-Lieve-Vrouwekerk.

462 **CHARLES THE BOLD**
AT: ONZE-LIEVE-VROUWEKERK
Mariastraat
Historic Centre ②
+32 (0)50 44 87 11
visitbruges.be

Charles the Bold is believed to be buried next to his daughter Mary of Burgundy. But no one is sure. Killed during a siege in 1477, Charles was buried at Nancy in France. In 1550, his skeleton was brought to Bruges for burial under a tomb similar to his daughter's. But the skeleton could be anyone.

463 **FERRY DE GROS**
AT: SINT-JAKOBSKERK
Sint-Jakobsstraat
Historic Centre ①

A strange Renaissance chapel is tucked into a corner of the Sint-Jakobskerk. It was built by Ferry de Gros after the death in 1521 of his first wife. The sculptor has placed husband and wife next to one another, but there is another woman lying below the couple. This was de Gros' second wife, who died in 1530.

464 **PIETER LANCHALS**
AT: ONZE-LIEVE-VROUWEKERK
Mariastraat
Historic Centre ②
+32 (0)50 44 87 11
visitbruges.be

The ornate tomb of Pieter Lanchals is decorated with his emblem, a swan (his name means "long neck" in Dutch). A city official, he was tortured and beheaded on Markt during the 1488 uprising because of his support for the unpopular Emperor Maximilian.

465 **FOUR UNKNOWN SOLDIERS**
Kleine Kerkhofstraat
Suburbs ⑦

The municipal cemetery contains graves of 15 unknown soldiers from WWI. But four are different, for they contain the graves of four of the five unknown soldiers brought to Bruges station from different World War One battlefields. One body was randomly chosen as the official Unknown Soldier, and reburied in Brussels. The other four were forgotten for many years, until a local journalist tracked them down in 2014.

463 FERRY DE GROS

The 5 people who
MADE BRUGES GREAT

466 JAN BREYDEL
Markt
Historic Centre ②

Club Brugge's football stadium is named after the early 14th-century hero Jan Breydel. His statue stands in the middle of Markt along with his companion Pieter de Coninck. They led a ragged army in 1302 that defeated French knights at the Battle of the Golden Spurs. The statue was carved in 1887.

466 JAN BREYDEL

467 LODEWIJK VAN GRUUTHUSE

Dijver 17-C
Historic Centre ②
+32 (0)50 44 87 43
visitbruges.be

A knight of the Order of the Golden Fleece, Lodewijk van Gruuthuse sold weapons, collected rare manuscripts and built an impressive palace in the centre of Bruges. His guests included King Edward IV of England, who stayed here with his brother Richard from October 1470 to April 1471.

468 SIMON STEVIN

Simon Stevinplein
Historic Centre ②

The shady square Simon Stevinplein is named after a scientist born in Bruges in about 1548. He was the first to use the decimal point, designed military fortifications and invented a sand yacht. The statue in the middle of the square shows Stevin holding a sketch of his famous yacht that could reach a speed of 35 km/h with 28 people on board.

469 KING LEOPOLD II

In a speech he delivered in 1877, King Leopold II called for Bruges "to restore its old and ancient monuments to create another Nuremberg". He went on to express his desire for "the entire city to be turned into a huge and splendid museum which no visitor to Belgium could fail to visit." As usual, the king got his way.

470 FRANK VAN ACKER

Vismarkt
Historic Centre ②

A statue on the waterfront commemorates Frank Van Acker who was appointed mayor in 1977. He launched ambitious plans to restore the historic city by cleaning up the stinking canals and replacing tarmac with cobblestones.

SWANS

30 RANDOM FACTS AND URBAN DETAILS

The 5

ODDEST SIGHTS

471 **DUMERY BELL**
Boeveriestraat
't Zand Quarter ⑥

Located on a little square not far from 't Zand, the mysterious Dumery bell hangs in a massive wooden frame. Cast in the 18th century at Joris Dumery's bell foundry, which stood near this spot, the 700 kg bell originally hung in the Belfry. It is now rung five times a year for ten minutes.

472 **THE LOST RIVER**
Jan van Eyckplein
Historic Centre ①

A river once ran from the Dampoort to Markt, but the stretch along Kraanrei has been covered over. The course of the hidden river is revealed by 13 cast iron manhole covers marked with a Gothic B for Bruges near the statue of Jan van Eyck.

473 **SMEDENPOORT SKULL**
Smedenstraat 71
't Zand Quarter ⑥

Look closely at the Smedenpoort and you will spot a metal skull embedded in the wall. It dates back to the 17th century when Louis XIV was about to attack Bruges. A Ghent man tried to let the enemy into the city, but his plan was discovered and he was beheaded. His skull was displayed on the gate as a warning and later replaced by a metal copy.

474 WOODEN CRANE

Wulpenstraat
Sint-Gillis Quarter ③

A replica mediaeval crane stands near the Dampoort in northern Bruges. The impressive crane was built by carpentry students at a local technical college in 2002. It is an exact copy of the old city crane originally sited on the Kraanplaats, even including the little wooden bird perched on the top.

475 COUPURE ARTWORK

Coupure
Historic Centre ②
kwaadbloed.com

The Brussels choreographer Ugo Dehaes created an artwork in 2002 next to a new bridge across the Coupure canal. Named c/o/u/p/u/r/e, it features a suspended wooden figure divided into separate sections supported by wires. The model is activated by a movement detector attached to a nearby tree, but you may have to wait some time before anything happens.

474 WOODEN CRANE

The 5 most

UNEXPECTED ANIMALS

476 **BEAR**
Academiestraat 14
Historic Centre ①

The statue of a bear on the wall of the 15th-century Poortersloge is described as the oldest citizen of Bruges. It refers to a mediaeval legend in which the Count of Flanders, Baldwin of the Iron Arm, killed a white bear in the woods near Bruges. Ever since, the bear has been the symbol of the city.

477 **DOG**
Groenerei
Historic Centre ②

Until he died in 2016, a Golden Retriever called Fidèle was the most famous dog in Belgium. He could be spotted with his head resting on an old pillow on the window ledge of the Côté Canal guesthouse overlooking the Groenerei canal. He even had a small role in the film *In Bruges*.

478 SWANS

Wijngaardplein
Begijnhof Quarter ⑤

It is often said that Emperor Maximilian punished the people of Bruges for executing his loyal official Pieter Lanchals by ordering them to keep 52 swans on the canals of Bruges. It is an unlikely story, since there were swans in Bruges long before Maximilian, but the legend is too romantic to go away.

479 SHEEP

Langerei 75
Sint-Gillis Quarter ③

Dogs you expect. But not sheep. You find them grazing in the little Hof de Jonghe park, and along the Damse Vaart leading to Damme. Every year, a herd of sheep is brought to Bruges to join the Holy Blood Procession and occasionally one or two will wander off into a local shop.

480 HORSES

Horses pulling carriages are a familiar sight in the streets of Bruges. They slow down the traffic and annoy local residents. Some would like them banned, but their owners point out the horses are kept in luxurious stables located in the farmland outside Bruges where they are given showers and two days of rest for each day they spend taking tourists around.

5 SURPRISING DATES
in Bruges' history

481 **3 JULY 1468**

On this day, Charles the Bold married Margaret of York in Damme, followed by ten days of celebrations in Bruges. One of the most fabulous weddings in history, it is commemorated every five years in the Procession of the Golden Tree.

482 **20 SEPTEMBER 1949**
Dijver 9
Historic Centre ②
coleurope.eu

The College of Europe was established in 1949 in a handsome building overlooking Dijver. Created by Europe's founding fathers soon after the end of the Second World War, its aim was to provide a postgraduate education for Europe's future leaders. It now occupies several historic buildings dotted around the city.

483 **21 SEPTEMBER 1988**

On this day, British Prime Minister Margaret Thatcher addressed the College of Europe in the great cloth hall below the Belfry. The speech shocked the audience with its anti-EU message and led to the creation of the powerful Bruges Group dedicated to taking Britain out of the European Union.

484 **20 FEBRUARY 2002**

Bruges began its year as cultural capital of Europe with ambitious projects to revitalise the city. The plans included contemporary architecture, poetry in public places and modern sculpture. The legacy of 2002 includes the Concertgebouw, the Conzett Bridge and poetry on house walls.

485 **9 MAY 2005**

On this day, Spencer Tunick photographed 700 naked people standing in the municipal theatre as part of the arts festival Corpus 05. Later in the day, he organised a photoshoot in which almost 2000 participants lay down in Vlamingstraat. He rounded off the wet and windy day by photographing 270 naked women in a procession of tourist boats.

The 5 streets to take to
AVOID THE CROWDS

486 **PHILIPSTOCKSTRAAT**
Philipstockstraat
Historic Centre ①

Bruges can sometimes seem impossibly crowded, but you can easily find quiet alternative routes. The narrow lane Breidelstraat, linking the main squares Markt and Burg, is often jammed with tourists, but there is a quiet route along Philipstockstraat. From here Burgstraat takes you to Burg through a quiet park.

487 **HALLESTRAAT**
Hallestraat
Historic Centre ②

The narrow Wollestraat is often crowded with tourists struggling to get from Markt to the beautiful Rozenhoedkaai. But there is another route that avoids the crush. Take the quiet lane Hallestraat to the right of the cloth hall and keep on straight ahead down the almost deserted Kartuizerinnenstraat. This will bring you out near the Rozenhoedkaai.

488 **GROENINGE**
Groeninge
Historic Centre ②

The Katelijnestraat is a busy route into Bruges packed with people and traffic. But if you are trying to get from Dijver to the Begijnhof, you can take the quiet lane Groeninge and then turn down Kastanjeboomstraat, avoiding the chaos.

489 ARSENAALSTRAAT

Arsenaalstraat
Begijnhof Quarter ⑤

Wijngaardstraat is a narrow lane used by tourists to reach the Begijnhof. But you don't need to fight through the crowds. There is an alternative route, not much longer, along the quiet Arsenaalstraat, leading to a quiet entrance into the Begijnhof.

490 HEILIGE-GEESTSTRAAT

Heilige-Geeststraat
Historic Centre ②

Most people head down Mariastraat to get from the Begijnhof quarter to the shopping district around Simon Stevinplein, but the peaceful alternative is to turn down the Heilige-Geeststraat, walk around the back of the Cathedral and follow Sint-Salvatorskoorstraat into Simon Stevinplein. You will hardly meet anyone.

486 PHILIPSTOCKSTRAAT

5 QUIET BENCHES

with the best views

491 GROENEREI
OPPOSITE:
Groenerei 2
Historic Centre ②

The city is dotted with green wooden benches supported on ornamental iron dragons. You find one of the benches shaded by a lime tree on the Groenerei canal, not far from a spot where Churchill liked to paint when he came to Bruges.

492 PREDIKHERENREI
FACING:
Predikherenrei 1
Sint-Anna Quarter ④

A single green bench stands on the Predikherenrei waterfront in front of the Uilenspiegel restaurant. It has a fabulous view facing down the Groenerei canal towards the Belfry. Shaded by an old plane tree, it is the perfect spot to sit on a quiet day in autumn.

493 AUGUSTIJNENREI
FACING:
Augustijnenrei 11
Historic Centre ①

A row of green dragon benches shaded by six lime trees stand on the Augustijnenrei canal. Only a few tourists ever come here, yet it is a beautiful spot near an ancient stone bridge. The perfect place to eat a sandwich.

494 **'T ZAND STEPS**
NEXT TO:
Concertgebouw
't Zand 34
't Zand Quarter ⑥

The square 't Zand was totally redesigned in 2016-2018 by a team led by Dutch architects West 8. They created a vast open space with plain concrete benches and some young trees. The architects also added two flights of sitting steps that run down to the hidden Kapucijnenrei canal. Locals like to gather in this romantic spot on summer evenings.

495 **VLAMINGBRUG**
NEAR:
Sint-Jorisstraat 1
Historic Centre ①

The old stone bridge on Vlamingstraat has low benches cut into the parapet. Historians believe they were used by merchants as shelves to display cloth and other goods. But now they are just spots to sit in the sun.

The 5 strangest
URBAN LEGENDS

496 **THE BRUGES MERIDIAN**
Markt 15
Historic Centre ②

Not many people notice the line of brass studs laid out on Markt between the Meridian 3 restaurant and Brasserie De Carré. They are aligned with a gold sphere on the top of the 15th-century Huis Bouchoute to create a kind of sundial that indicates noon. This curious invention was one of ten installed in Belgium in 1836 to harmonise clocks across the country and help people catch trains.

497 **THE PLAGUE OF FROGS**
OPPOSITE:
Dijver 4
Historic Centre ②

The sculptors Depuydt and Canestraro created more than 20 modern bronze statues in Bruges in the 1980s. Some conceal a hidden frog, including *De Geliefden* (The Lovers) on Burg and *De Bloementuil* (The Flower Basket) on Dijver, which has four little frogs hidden among the flowers. Children enjoy hunting for the frogs, but a local artist has called for the sculptures to be removed.

498 THE SECRET POEM

't Zand 34
't Zand Quarter ⑥
+32 (0)50 47 69 99
concertgebouw.be

The poet Peter Verhelst created a long poem for the Concertgebouw in 2002. It was split into fragments to be placed on the backs of the 1300 chairs in the main concert hall. The poem has never been published, so it can only be read by walking slowly through the concert hall.

499 THE GHOST HOUSE

Spanjaardstraat 17
Historic Centre ①

The house at Spanjaardstraat 17 stands on the site of a nunnery once linked by a secret tunnel to a monastery. According to an old legend, a lovestruck Italian monk used the tunnel one night in 1498 to pursue a nun. When she rejected him, he killed her in a fit of rage. Her ghost is said to wander through the building at night.

500 IF YOU LEAVE

Bargeweg 2
Begijnhof Quarter ⑤

The town is dotted with poems placed in public spots in 2002 when Bruges was cultural capital of Europe. One was written on the whitewashed wall of the waterfront Bargehuis, where brightly-decorated barges left for Ghent up until the 19th century. 'If you leave, will you come back/If I come back, will you be there?' it reads.

"IF YOU LEAVE" – WILL YOU RETURN?

DUO

INDEX

COLOPHON

EDITING *and* COMPOSING – Derek Blyth

GRAPHIC DESIGN — Joke Gossé and Sarah Schrauwen

PHOTOGRAPHY — Roel Hendrickx — roelh.zenfolio.com

COVER IMAGE — DEPOT d'O (secret 201)

The addresses in this book have been selected after thorough independent research by the author, in collaboration with Luster Publishers. The selection is solely based on personal evaluation of the business by the author. Nothing in this book was published in exchange for payment or benefits of any kind.

D/2018/12.005/18

ISBN 978 94 6058 2325

NUR 511, 510

www.lusterweb.com — www.the500hiddensecrets.com

info@lusterweb.com

Printed in Italy by Printer Trento.

FSC
www.fsc.org
MIX
Paper from responsible sources
FSC® C015829